westermann

CAMDEN MARKET

7

Grammatiktrainer

CAMDEN MARKET 7

Grammatiktrainer

Autoren: Robert Klimmt (Leipzig), Jutta Stahl-Klimmt (Leipzig)

Zusatzmaterialien zu Camden Market 7

Materialien für Lehrerinnen und Lehrer

- Textbook für Lehrkräfte 7 (ISBN 978-3-14-149149-4)
- Materialien für Lehrkräfte 7 (ISBN 978-3-14-149150-0)
- Differenzierende Kopiervorlagen 7
  (ISBN 978-3-14-149155-5)
- Lernerfolgskontrollen 7 (ISBN 978-3-14-149152-4)
- CD für Lehrkräfte 7 (ISBN 978-3-14-149153-1)
- DVD für Lehrkräfte 7 (ISBN 978-3-14-149154-8)
- Online-Diagnose zu Camden Market 7
  www.onlinediagnose.de

Materialien für Schülerinnen und Schüler

- Textbook 7 (ISBN 978-3-14-149138-8)
- Workbook 7 (ISBN 978-3-14-149139-5)
- Workbook 7 mit interaktiven Übungen
  (ISBN 978-3-14-145282-2)
- Interaktive Übungen 7 (ISBN 978-3-14-149368-9)
- Arbeitsbuch Inklusion 7 (ISBN 978-3-14-149141-8)
- Klassenarbeitstrainer 7 (ISBN 978-3-14-149142-5)
- Wortschatztrainer 7 (ISBN 978-3-14-149392-4)
- Let's talk 7 (ISBN 978-3-14-149146-3)
- Let's write 7 (ISBN 978-3-14-149402-0)
- Westermann Vokabeltrainer-App zu Camden Market 7
  www.westermann.de/vokabeltrainer

Das digitale Schulbuch und digitale Unterrichtsmaterialien für Schülerinnen und Schüler und
für Lehrkräfte finden Sie in der BiBox – dem digitalen Unterrichtssystem passend zum Lehrwerk.
Mehr Informationen über aktuelle Lizenzen finden Sie auf www.bibox.schule.

www.westermann.de/camden-market

© 2022 Bildungshaus Schulbuchverlage Westermann Schroedel Diesterweg Schöningh Winklers GmbH,
Georg-Westermann-Allee 66, 38104 Braunschweig
www.westermann.de

Druck A² / Jahr 2025
Alle Drucke der Serie A sind im Unterricht parallel verwendbar.

Die Seiten dieses Produkts bestehen zu 100 % aus Altpapier.

Damit tragen wir dazu bei, dass Wald geschützt wird, Ressourcen geschont werden und der Einsatz von Chemikalien reduziert wird. Die Produktion eines Klassensatzes unserer Arbeitshefte aus reinem Altpapier spart durchschnittlich 12 Kilogramm Holz und 178 Liter Wasser, sie vermeidet 7 Kilogramm Abfall und reduziert den Ausstoß von Kohlendioxid im Vergleich zu einem Klassensatz aus Frischfaserpapier. Unser Recyclingpapier ist nach den Richtlinien des Blauen Engels zertifiziert.

Redaktion: Nathalie Heiniger
Illustrationen: Carla Miller, Unna
Layout: JANSSEN KAHLERT Design & Kommunikation GmbH, Hannover
Umschlaggestaltung: LIO Design GmbH, Braunschweig
Druck und Bindung: Westermann Druck GmbH, Georg-Westermann-Allee 66, 38104 Braunschweig

ISBN 978-3-14-**149143**-2

Willkommen beim neuen Grammatiktrainer!

Liebe Schülerin, lieber Schüler, liebe Eltern,

wer eine fremde Sprache lernt, will andere Menschen verstehen können und von ihnen verstanden werden. Wir treten heute mit vielen Menschen aus unterschiedlichen Ländern in Kontakt – in unserer Familie, im Internet oder im Berufsleben. Mit diesen möchten wir gerne kommunizieren. Dabei hat sich Englisch als weltweite Verkehrssprache etabliert und begegnet uns im Alltag ständig.

Wenn wir eine Fremdsprache lernen, dann wird oft auf grammatische Formen und Strukturen verwiesen. Die sprachlichen Mittel dienen uns dazu, bestimmte Sprechabsichten auszudrücken. Sie machen z. B. den Unterschied zwischen Gegenwart, Vergangenheit und Zukunft aus.

In unserer Muttersprache wenden wir Grammatik erst einmal unbewusst an. In der Fremdsprache benötigen wir grammatische Strukturen für einen systematischen und ganzheitlichen Spracherwerb. Darüber hinaus fördert das Erlernen dieser grammatischen Strukturen den Aufbau eines allgemeinen Sprachlernbewusstseins, welches uns beim Lernen weiterer Sprachen hilft.

Der Fokus in diesem Heft liegt darauf, dass bestimmte Sprechabsichten in Englisch umgesetzt werden können. Die Funktion der Grammatik steht also immer im Vordergrund. Wir möchten dir dabei helfen, dass du dich in der englischen Sprache sicher ausdrücken und dies auch in der Schule zeigen kannst. Daher sind die Kapitel systematisch aufgebaut. Es ist dabei wie beim Sport: Man fängt erst mal klein an und trainiert dann nach dem Motto „Übung macht den Meister"!

Wir wünschen viel Spaß und Erfolg bei der Arbeit mit dem Grammatiktrainer!

Aufbau der Kapitel

Die Kapitel im Grammatiktrainer sind wie folgt aufgebaut:

Introduction

Die Einleitung besteht aus einem kurzen Text und einem Bild. Die dargestellte Situation zeigt anhand eines Beispiels, wofür die grammatische Struktur verwendet wird.

Language Tip

Der *Language Tip* fasst kurz zusammen, welche Funktion die grammatische Struktur erfüllt und wie sie gebildet wird. Für fast alle Kapitel gibt es auch ein Video, in dem die Bildung der Grammatik erklärt wird. Du findest es mit dem Webcode, der unter dem *Language Tip* steht. Damit kannst du noch einmal wiederholen, was du im Unterricht schon gelernt hast oder auch schon etwas vorarbeiten.

▷ Gehe auf unsere Webseite und gib den passenden Webcode ein: **https://www.westermann.de/webcode**

Du kannst die Videos auch auf einem Tablet oder Smartphone abspielen.

Language Detective

Jetzt bist du an der Reihe! Beim *Language Detective* gehst du selbst auf Spurensuche und findest die grammatischen Strukturen im Einleitungstext. Die Lösungen findest du im Lösungsanhang. Dort kannst du sie eigenständig kontrollieren.

Exercises

Die *Exercises* sind so angeordnet, dass die Aufgaben schrittweise immer offener werden, bis du ganze Sätze in der neuen Grammatik bilden kannst. Dabei empfiehlt es sich, die Lösungen nach jeder Aufgabe im Lösungsanhang zu kontrollieren, damit sich keine Fehler einschleichen. Aber keine Angst vor Fehlern: sie sind ein wichtiger Bestandteil des Lernens!

Over to you

Bei der *Over-to-you* Aufgabe geht es nun darum, einen eigenen Text zu erstellen. So siehst du gleich, welche Sprechabsicht man nun in der englischen Sprache mithilfe der neuen Grammatik ausdrücken kann.
Vielleicht hast du ja einen englischsprachigen Bekannten, dem du dein neues Können zeigen willst? Dann schicke ihm doch eine Nachricht und warte, was er oder sie antwortet!

Unsere Tipps fürs Lernen:

Karteikarten

Karteikarten haben eine praktische Größe und lassen sich überall mit hinnehmen. Schreibe dir die Grammatik noch einmal auf Karteikarten. Notiere dir die Funktion, die Formel zur Bildung der Grammatik und ein paar Beispielsätze (positiv, negativ, Fragen) - das alles möglichst anschaulich, also z. B. mit verschiedenen Farben.

Der richtige Ort zum Lernen

Es ist gut, einen Ort zum Lernen und einen anderen Ort zum Ausruhen zu haben - also möglichst nicht auf dem Bett oder der Couch lernen. Vielleicht richtest du dir einen Platz ein, der möglichst wenige Ablenkungen bereit hält, aber dennoch bequem ist, dann klappt es mit der Konzentration schon viel besser!

Pausen sind wichtig

In der Schule hat man Pausen, um sich zwischen den Stunden zu erholen. Genauso wichtig sind Pausen auch, wenn du daheim lernst. Dein Gehirn kann nur so viele Informationen auf einmal abspeichern, danach braucht es eine Ruhezeit. Es ist auch sehr wichtig, dass du dann etwas Wasser trinkst und dir vielleicht einen kleinen Snack gönnst. So ist das Lernen gleich viel effizienter!

Gemeinsam lernen

Es ist wichtig, sich Zeit alleine zum konzentrierten Lernen zu nehmen. Gemeinsames Lernen ist aber auch sehr effektiv und kann für viele motivierender sein, als sich alleine hinzusetzen. Das kann mit Klassenkameraden, deinen Geschwistern, deinen Eltern oder anderen Verwandten sein. Erkläre ihnen doch einmal, was du gerade lernst oder lass dich von ihnen abhören. Gemeinsam schafft ihr das!

Und natürlich üben, üben, üben ... aber das tust du ja bereits mit dem Grammatiktrainer :-)!

Grüne Kapitel: Die Grammatik kommt im Challenge-Teil vor.

Introduction

This is me and my friend Bill. I want to tell you what a great sportsperson he is. He is the fastest runner at our school. He's even faster than our PE teacher. OK, I must say that it is more difficult for our PE teacher because she is also the oldest teacher in the school. When our PE teacher was younger, she was the most successful athlete at her school. When she was as old as we are now, she won more races than anybody else. My friend Bill wants to do more interesting things than just running. He thinks rugby is the most exciting sport of all. So, he joined our school's rugby team. I think he will become the best rugby player in the team.
I'll keep you posted!
Ellie

Language Tip

Mit Adjektiven kannst du Personen und Dinge beschreiben. Wenn du Personen oder Dinge **vergleichen** möchtest, kannst du Adjektive steigern. **Kurze Adjektive** (mit höchstens zwei Silben) steigerst du mit **-er** und **-est**. **Lange Adjektive** (mit drei oder mehr Silben) steigerst du mit *more* und *most*. Es gibt auch unregelmäßige Formen, die du lernen musst.

adjective	comparative	superlative	adjective	comparative	superlative
fit	fitter	(the) fittest	famous	more famous	(the) most famous
pretty	prettier	(the) prettiest	successful	more successful	(the) most successful
good	better	(the) best	expensive	more expensive	(the) most expensive

Wenn du ungleiche Dinge miteinander vergleichen möchtest, benutzt du den **Komparativ** und *than*. Wenn du gleiche Dinge miteinander vergleichen möchtest, verwendest du *as ... as*.

Beispiele: Tennis is **easier than** football.   Tim is **as tall as** Sophie.

  Grammatikvideo: **WES-149143-001**

Language Detective

a) Highlight all **comparatives** in the **introduction** in green and all **superlatives** in red.
b) Find the right English expressions:

1. der schnellste Läufer der Schule _____

2. so alt wie wir sind _____

3. interessantere Dinge als Laufen _____

EXERCISE Faster

1 Records

Comparative or superlative? Circle the right words.

1. Basketballers are usually **taller / the tallest** than footballers.
2. Hockey is probably **faster / the fastest** sport in the world.
3. Marathon runners are **slower / the slowest** than sprinters.
4. Rugby players are often **heavier / the heaviest** than horse riders.
5. Boxing might be **more difficult / the most difficult** sport in the world.
6. Football players are often **more famous / the most famous** than athletes.
7. Basketball player LeBron James has been named **fitter / the fittest** athlete in the world.

2 Let's compare!

a) What does the PE teacher say? Write comparisons with **than**.

1. A basketball is _bigger than_ _____ (big) a golf ball, and a

   football is _____ (heavy) a tennis ball.

2. Next year we will all be _____ (fit)

   this year because we will train very hard.

3. Cycling is _____ (easy) skateboarding.

4. Rugby is _____ (dangerous) yoga.

5. Our rugby team is _____ (successful) the football team.

6. Some swimmers are famous, but football players are usually _____

   (famous) swimmers.

7. There are _____ (many) players in our football team at school

   _____ in our rugby team.

b) What do YOU think? Compare the two things with **than**. Use the adjectives in brackets.

1. football – tennis (interesting): _____

2. PE lessons – maths lessons (good): _____

3. hockey – ice hockey (difficult): _____

3 Bigger and better

What do the classmates say during the PE lesson? Fill in the **comparative** or **superlative** of the adjectives.

1. Wow, she was so fast , even _____ than Eric. And he is _____

   _____ boy in his class. **(fast)**

2. I think that volleyball is the _____ sport.

   It is definitely _____ than yoga! **(exciting)**

3. Do you know the name of _____ basketball player ever? **(successful)**

4. Jumping off a cliff is _____ than jumping into a pool. **(dangerous)**

5. Some days are just bad days. But yesterday was _____ day in my life. It just

   can't get any _____ than that. **(bad)**

4 Bernie and Sandy

Look at the fact files and compare Bernie and Sandy. Write sentences with the **comparative**.

Bernie

- 13 years old
- 1.62 m tall
- OK at school
- fit
- slow swimmer
- does two sports

Sandy

- 14 years old
- 1.64 m tall
- very good at school
- very fit
- fast swimmer
- does one sport

1. Bernie is younger than Sandy. / Sandy is older than Bernie. _____

2. _____

3. _____

4. _____

5. _____

6. _____

5 How do you say it in English?

Write the sentences in English.

1. Rugby ist gefährlicher als Schwimmen.

   _____

2. Kannst du die Luft länger als zwei Minuten anhalten[1]?

   _____

3. Fahrradfahren ist nicht so langweilig wie Laufen.

   _____

4. Wo ist der nächste Skatepark?

   _____

5. Er ist der erfolgreichste deutsche Fußballspieler.

   _____

Over to you

Write a short blog entry about sports. Compare different sports or players and write your opinion about them.
Use comparatives and superlatives. The words in the boxes can help you.

| rugby | running | dancing | swimming |
goalkeeper | field player | professional player | …

easy | difficult | boring | good |
fast | slow | successful | famous | …

Hi guys! Today I am going to write about sports. First of all, I think the best sport

[1] Luft anhalten: *to hold one's breath*

Introduction

I am really looking forward to visiting my granny. I must say that my grandma is very special. The only problem with my granny is that she keeps telling everybody what food they should and shouldn't eat.
I am not allowed to have any coke at her house and she keeps telling me that I mustn't bring any of those energy drinks. She says that shops shouldn't be allowed to sell them to teenagers. I also can't eat fast food. I have to eat healthy food. Well, my granny can cook very well and I really enjoy her home cooked meals, but I miss sweets. How can people live without sweets? I really don't know … I have to sneak in[1] some chocolate bars. I have to eat them when she is asleep. What about your grandma?

Language Tip

Mit **Modalverben** (Modal = Art und Weise) kannst du ausdrücken, was jemand **(nicht) kann**, **(nicht) darf**, **(nicht) machen soll** oder **(nicht) machen muss**.

Ist etwas **erlaubt** oder **möglich**, so kannst du *can* (können) sowie die Ersatzformen *be allowed to* (dürfen) oder *be able to* (die Fähigkeit haben) verwenden. **Verbote** drückst du mit *can't* (nicht können) und *not be allowed to* (nicht dürfen) aus. Mit *must not* drückst du ein **starkes Verbot** aus.

Beispiele: I **can** eat sweets.   He **wasn't allowed to** drink coke.

> Achtung:
> *Must not (mustn't)*
> klingt wie nicht müssen,
> heißt aber <u>nicht dürfen</u>!

Must heißt **müssen**. Meist kannst du es auch durch *have to / has to* ersetzen. Wenn du sagen willst, dass jemand etwas **nicht tun muss**, verwendest du *don't / doesn't have to*. Mit *should* (sollen) und *should not* (nicht sollen) drückst du eine **Empfehlung** aus.

Beispiele: I **have to** eat healthy food.   We **shouldn't** eat so much sugar.

 Grammatikvideo: **WES-149143-002**

Language Detective

a) Highlight all **modal verbs** in the **introduction**. Use green for the ones that tell you that you can do something and red for the ones that tell you that you can't do something.
b) Find the right English expressions for:

1. Ich darf keine Cola in ihrem Haus trinken. _____

2. Ich darf keine Energy Drinks mitbringen. _____

3. Ich darf auch kein Fast Food essen. _____

1 sneak in: *hereinschmuggeln*

1 Can or can't?

Circle the right words.

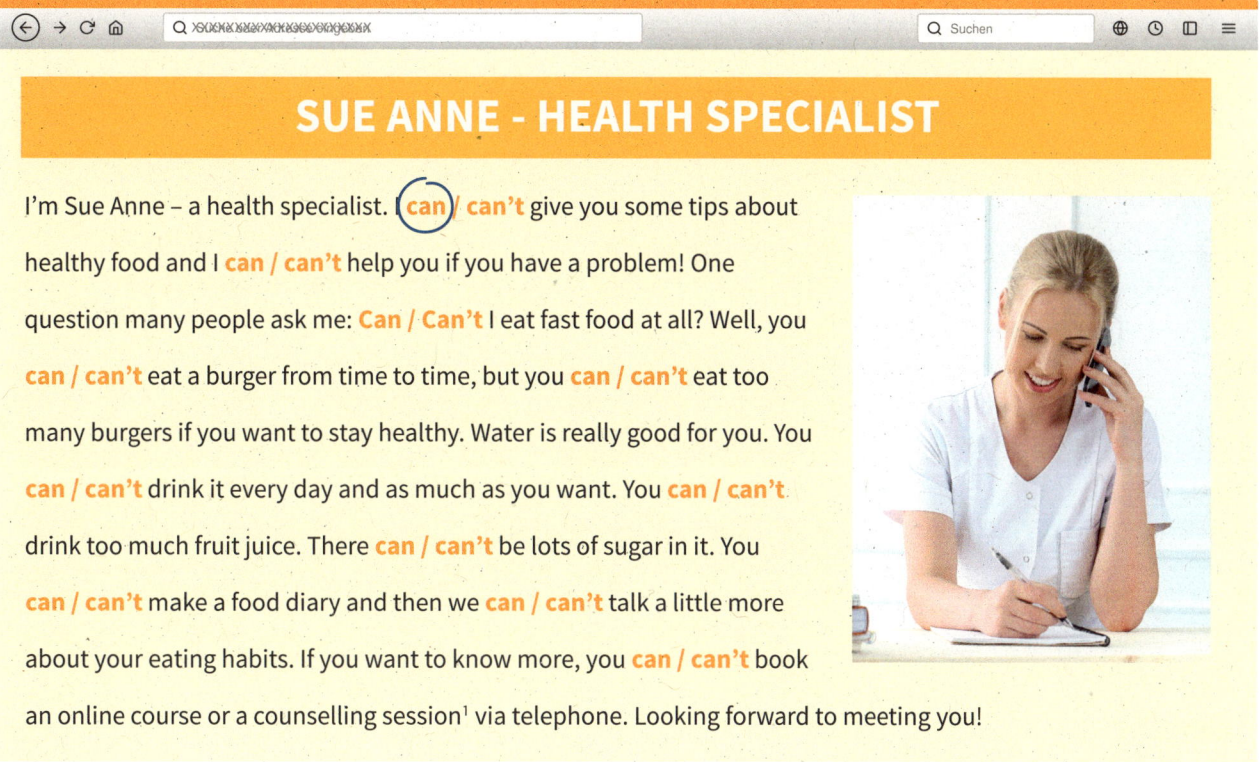

SUE ANNE - HEALTH SPECIALIST

I'm Sue Anne – a health specialist. I **can** / **can't** give you some tips about healthy food and I **can** / **can't** help you if you have a problem! One question many people ask me: **Can** / **Can't** I eat fast food at all? Well, you **can** / **can't** eat a burger from time to time, but you **can** / **can't** eat too many burgers if you want to stay healthy. Water is really good for you. You **can** / **can't** drink it every day and as much as you want. You **can** / **can't** drink too much fruit juice. There **can** / **can't** be lots of sugar in it. You **can** / **can't** make a food diary and then we **can** / **can't** talk a little more about your eating habits. If you want to know more, you **can** / **can't** book an online course or a counselling session[1] via telephone. Looking forward to meeting you!

2 Mum …

What do Yusuf and his mother say? Fill the gaps with the right modal verbs from the box.

> can | can't | should | shouldn't | must | have to | not have to | mustn't

Mum: You _____ put so much sugar into your tea.

Yusuf: Mum, you _____ tell me what to do.

Why don't you sit next to me and then we _____ finish eating our toast?

Mum: Your teeth don't look very good. I think you _____ brush them more often.

Yusuf: Do I really _____ eat all the vegetables at dinner today?

Mum: I think you _____ eat them. Vegetables are good for you.

Please listen, you _____ take all your medicine today.

It _____ be very dangerous for you if you don't.

Now hurry up. You _____ be late for school today!

---

1 counselling session: *Beratungsgespräch*

3 What are they allowed to do?

Write sentences with (**not**) **be allowed to**.

1
Ben, you know the rule: no sweets before dinner!

2
Sorry boys, but no pets in our shop!

3
Of course, Gina. Your friends are welcome to come to our house!

4
OK, you can have some coke. But only one can.

5
Jasmine, please! No music after ten o'clock!

6
You can use your mobile phones for your presentation.

1. Ben is not allowed to eat sweets before dinner.

2. _____

3. _____

4. _____

5. _____

6. _____

4 How do you say it in English?

Write the right English sentences.

1. Du solltest nicht zu viel Zucker essen.

_____

2. Der Hund darf auf keinen Fall Schokolade essen. Das ist schlecht für ihn.

_____

3. Dürfen wir den Kuchen essen?

_____

4. Wir müssen die Milch nicht trinken.

_____

5. Sie darf keine Cola trinken.

_____

Over to you

Make a poster about healthy eating habits with five rules or suggestions. You can use the ideas from the box. Draw pictures for the rules, too. Example: "You can eat some fast food, but you shouldn't eat too much of it."

- What can you eat / drink a lot of?
- What should you not eat very often?
- How much sugar or fat can you eat?
- What should you never eat or drink?
- What can you put into your lunch box?

Introduction

Hi! This is Tabea from Germany. Today I want to talk about German food. Have you ever eaten traditional German food? I am sure you have heard about schnitzel and bratwurst. The English language has already adopted[1] these words – also pretzel (from the German "Brezel") and sauerkraut. My friend Kieran from England has tried all these food. He especially enjoys our bread. He says he has never been to a country where they have so many different kinds of bread, but he hasn't had "Pumpernickel" yet. That is a special kind of bread which is very dark. We also eat lots of international food. I have never been to a German city where there is not at least one Italian, Turkish and Greek restaurant. Asian food has also become very popular. Have you ever tried Sushi?

Language Tip

Das *present perfect* verwendest du, wenn etwas irgendwann, noch nie oder noch nicht geschehen ist oder wenn eine Handlung in der Vergangenheit **Auswirkungen auf die Gegenwart** hat.

Vergangenheit   Gegenwart   Zukunft

Du bildest das *present perfect* mit *have* oder *has* und dem **Partizip Perfekt (der 3. Form des Verbs)**. Bei der Verneinung stellst du ein *not* hinter *have / has* oder verwendest eine Kurzform. Bei Fragen stellst du *have* oder *has* an den Satzanfang bzw. hinter das Fragewort.

Aussagesatz:	I **have eaten** lots of German food.
Verneinung:	I **have not tried** sushi.
Fragen:	**Have** you **been** to the Greek restaurant?
	Why have you **eaten** all the cake?

Partizip Perfekt:
Bei **regelmäßigen Verben** hängst du ein **-ed** an, um das Partizip Perfekt zu bilden. Unregelmäßige Formen musst du lernen.

 Grammatikvideo: **WES-149143-003**

Language Detective

a) Highlight all **verbs** in the **introduction** which are in the **present perfect**.
b) Find the right English expressions for:

1. Habt ihr schon mal deutsches Essen gegessen? _____

2. Er hat noch nie Pumpernickel gegessen. _____

3. Ich war noch nie in einer deutschen Stadt, die … _____

4. Habt ihr schon mal Sushi probiert? _____

1 adopted: *übernommen*

EXERCISE Have you ever tried Sushi?

1 Choose!

These are pictures from Kieran's social media account. What are the right captions? Tick the correct sentences.

☐ I have never eat sushi.

☐ I have never eaten sushi.

☐ They have never tried Haggis.

☐ They has never tried Haggis.

☐ Has you ever baking a cake?

☐ Have you ever baked a cake?

☐ She has never been to Italy.

☐ She have never been to Italy.

2 Food and drinks

a) Fill in the **past participle** of the verbs.

infinitive	past participle
order	ordered
eat	
cut	
forget	
try	
cook	
finish	
drink	

b) What do Kieran's family members say? Complete the sentences with the verbs from a). Use the **present perfect**.

1. This soup isn't very tasty. I _____ to put in the salt.

2. Can you smell that? Dad _____ dinner. Yummy!

3. We _____ some water for you. The waiter was just here.

4. Sorry, there is no more chocolate left. Dad _____ it all.

5. I _____ frog legs. I think they're really good.

6. Who _____ the tomatoes? The pieces are so small!

7. Our cat _____ too much cat milk. That's not good for them.

8. Sarah _____ her dinner and wants to go to her room now.

3 | Answers

Write the answers in the **present perfect**.

1. "That smells good!" I – make – some pizza. ___I have made some pizza.___

2. "He can't sleep." He – drink – too much coke. _____

3. "Is this vegetarian?" Yes – I – not put in – meat. _____

4. "Have we got muesli?" No – I – not buy – any muesli. _____

5. "Are they still there?" No – they – already – leave. _____

4 | I haven't done it.

Finish the sentences with the words in brackets. Use the **present perfect**.

1. Colin has already finished his meal, but I ___haven't finished mine yet_____

   (not finish mine yet).

2. They have enjoyed the chili con carne, but Kieran _____

   (not enjoy it). It was too hot for him.

3. My sister has already been to many restaurants, but I _____

   (never be to a Greek restaurant).

4. A very good restaurant has opened in our street, but we _____

   _____ (not have dinner there yet).

5. My grandparents like fish, but they _____ (never order) sushi.

5 | Questions

Write questions in the **present perfect**.

1. she – ever – try – fish and chips? _____

2. Timmy – ever – drink – sparkling water? _____

3. you – ever – make chocolate cookies? _____

4. where – he – learn to cook this? _____

5. why – they – not started their dinner? _____

6. how – you – do it? _____

6 What has happened?

Write one sentence for each picture. Use the **present perfect**.

1. _____

2. _____

3. _____

4. _____

Over to you

Write a blog entry about what you have done or not done yet when it comes to food. Ask your readers at least three questions about food. Use the present perfect and time words such as yet, already, never and always. You can use the ideas in the list, or use your own ideas. Write at least 8 sentences.

- go to an expensive restaurant
- try sushi / frog legs / insect pasta
- drink sugary drinks
- have lunch at school
- have a burger for breakfast
- buy fresh food at a market
- cook a healthy dinner
- order a vegan dish

Hey everyone!

_____

_____

_____

_____

_____

_____

_____

_____

Introduction

Waitress: Welcome to our seafood restaurant. May I take your order?
Dad: How many dishes do you have? The menu is huge.
Waitress: Wow, I don't really know. There must be more than a hundred, but our cooks can make so much more food. Not only the ones on the menu. Sheila can make lots of soups.
Dad: OK. I think I will go for the fish burger.
Waitress: How many burgers would you like to order?
Dad: Well, we will have two seafood burgers and one fish burger for my son or is the burger too much for a child?
Waitress: Yes, I think so. I would recommend fish nuggets.
Dad: Thanks so much. My daughter doesn't like fish or seafood very much. What would you recommend[1] for her?
Waitress: We have so many different kinds of chips – potato, sweet potato or vegetable chips, for example.
Dad: OK. I think we might need a few more minutes.

Language Tip

Much (viel), *many* (viele) und *a lot of* (viel, viele) sind Mengenangaben, die man zusammen mit Nomen im Plural verwendet. Hierbei machst du einen Unterschied zwischen bejahten und verneinten Aussagen und Fragen.

In der Regel verwendest du *a lot of* (oder die informelle Variante *lots of*) in **bejahten Aussagesätzen**. Bei **Verneinungen und Fragen** verwendest du *many* für **zählbare Nomen** (z. B. *bottles, eggs*) und *much* für **nichtzählbare Nomen** (z. B. water, time).

Aussagesatz: **They ate a lot of seafood.**
Verneinung: **We didn't have much time to order.**
Fragen: **Do you have many dishes?**
     Did you eat much ice cream?

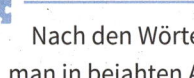 Nach den Wörtern **too** und **so** verwendet man in bejahten Aussagesätzen auch **much** und **many**, z. B. **There was <u>so</u> much cake.**

 Grammatikvideo: **WES-149143-004**

Language Detective

a) Highlight **much** and **many** in the **introduction**.
b) Underline all positive statements in green. Look at the ones with **much** und **many**. Which words are in front of them in positive statements? Highlight them.
c) Find the right English expressions for:

1. Wie viele Gerichte haben Sie? _____

2. Sheila kann viele Suppen machen. _____

3. Ist der Burger zu viel für ein Kind? _____

4. Vielen Dank! _____

[1] recommend: *empfehlen*

EXERCISE We've got so many dishes.

1 At the restaurant

What do the family members say at the restaurant? Cross out the wrong words.

1. Look at the man over there. How can he eat so **much / many** pizza?

2. How **much / many** bottles of water have you ordered?

3. Wow. There are so **much / many** dishes on the menu.

4. I think they have put too **much / many** eggs in the cake.

5. How **much / many** lemonade did you drink?

6. That dessert is too **much / many** for me.

2 Indian restaurant

Fill in the right words from the box.

| much | many | a lot of |

Q XXXXXXXXXXXXXXXXXXXXXX   Q Suchen

Taj Mahal Restaurant

Welcome to our restaurant. We offer you _____ different dishes from all over India.

We use _____ spices to make our food tasty. But at our restaurant, we don't use

_____ salt, because too _____ salt is not good for you. We can also

offer you some vegetarian food if you don't want to eat so _____ meat.

_____ people have already tasted our food and we have received so _____

good reviews. Please book a table online because we do not have so _____ tables. If

there are too _____ people here, we will have to send you away.

3 How do you say it in English?

Write the sentences in English.

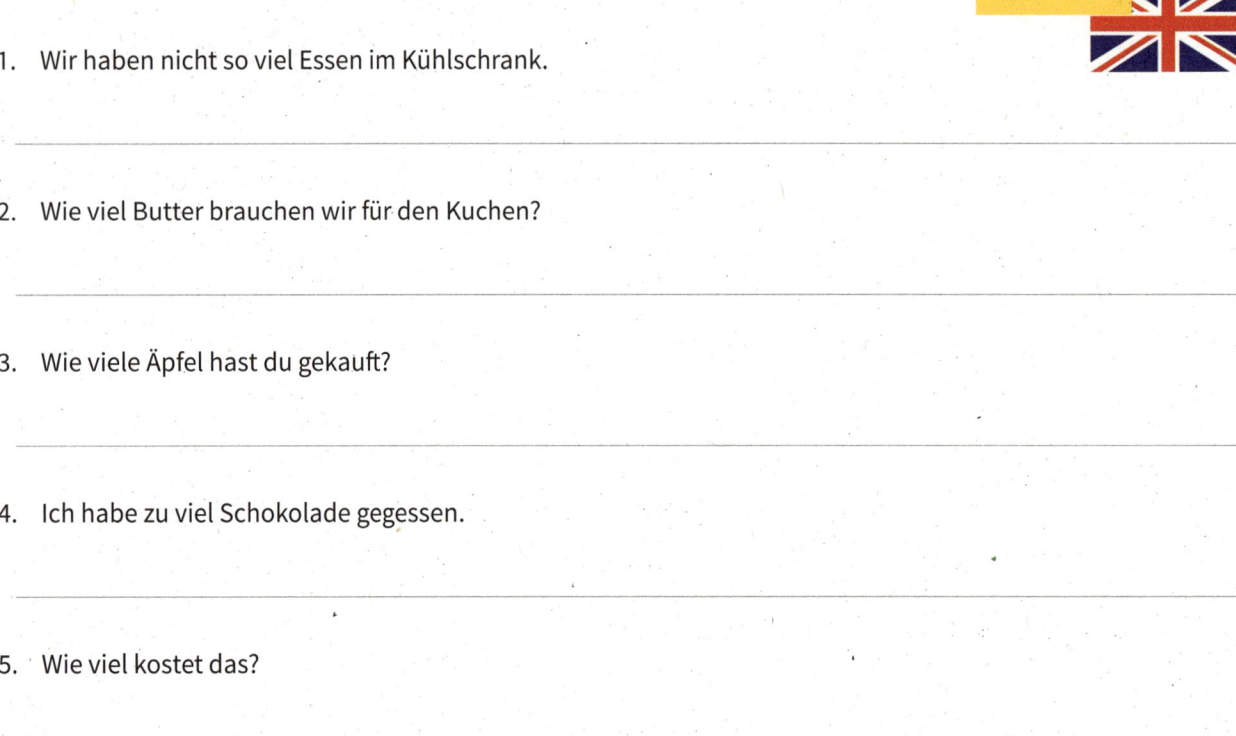

1. Wir haben nicht so viel Essen im Kühlschrank.

_____

2. Wie viel Butter brauchen wir für den Kuchen?

_____

3. Wie viele Äpfel hast du gekauft?

_____

4. Ich habe zu viel Schokolade gegessen.

_____

5. Wie viel kostet das?

_____

Over to you

You want to have a party with your friends at the weekend. Write an email to your friends to organise the food for the party. Who will bring what? What have you got at home? What food do you (not) like? Write at least eight sentences and use **much**, **many** and **a lot of**.

Hi everyone!

I want to talk about the food for our party. We are lots of people so we need lots of food.

_____

_____

_____

_____

_____

_____

Introduction

Ada: I'm OK with healthy food, but the fact that they don't sell any sweets in the cafeteria ... That's stupid, isn't it?

Emma: You're right, but you could put some sweets into your lunchbox, couldn't you?

Ada: Our head teacher told us not to bring any sweets, didn't he?

Emma: No, he didn't. I think he said that we were not allowed to sell any sweets. So, taking a chocolate bar to school should be OK, shouldn't it? If you eat it yourself I mean. I sometimes put one in my lunchbox and so far, I haven't been in any trouble yet, have I?

Ada: No, you haven't. Let's have a look at the menu for today.

Emma: Chicken Curry. That sounds great, doesn't it?

Ada: If it was a vegetarian curry ... I don't eat meat, do I?

Emma: No, you don't. How could I forget ... We can go outside and have lunch there. It's lovely weather, isn't it?

Language Tip

Wenn du wissen möchtest, ob dein Gesprächspartner dir bei einer Sache zustimmt, kannst du Bestätigungsfragen verwenden. Im Englischen nennt man sie *question tags*, also „Frageanhänger". Im Deutschen verwenden wir hierfür die Bezeichnungen „richtig?", „gell?", „oder?" und „nicht wahr?".

Du bildest das *question tag*, indem du das Hilfsverb aus dem Satz verwendest. Falls dort kein Hilfsverb steht, verwendest du *do/does* oder *did* – je nach Zeitform.

Bei einem **bejahenden Aussagesatz (+)** is das **question tag negativ (-)**
The food is great, isn't it?

Bei einem **verneinendem Aussagesatz (-)** ist das **question tag positiv (+)**,
He didn't eat all the cake, did he?

Als Antwort auf ein *question tag* verwendest du eine Kurzantwort, z. B. "Yes, it is". Ein reines "Yes." oder "No." gilt als unhöflich!

📹 Grammatikvideo: **WES-149143-005**

Language Detective

a) Highlight all positive **question tags** in the **introduction** in green and all negative ones in red.
b) Find the right English expressions for:

1. Das ist doof, nicht wahr? _____

2. Das hört sich gut an, gell? _____

3. Ich esse kein Fleisch, oder? _____

4. Nein, das tust du nicht. _____

1 ... is it?

Cross out the wrong **question tags**.

1. There is a cafeteria at the school, **is there/ isn't there**?

2. Sweets for breakfast isn't very healthy, **is it / isn't it**?

3. The vegetable dishes are quite expensive, **are they / aren't they**?

4. He has eaten a curry before, **has he / hasn't he**?

5. We shouldn't eat so much sugar, **should we / shouldn't we**?

6. You can bring your own food to the cafeteria, **can you / can't you**?

7. She didn't eat the meat, **did she / didn't she**?

8. They have never been to our cafeteria, **have they / haven't they**?

2 Healthy food

What do the classmates say? Fill in the right **question tags**.

1. This apple is delicious, _____?

2. You can bake good cakes, _____?

3. They offer a great variety of salads, _____?

4. We are allowed to bring a bottle of water, _____?

5. We aren't allowed to sell sweets to other students, _____?

6. Our lunchboxes should contain healthy food, _____?

7. Schools don't teach students enough about healthy eating, _____?

8. Last week Ben interviewed his classmates about school lunches, _____?

9. Amy didn't want to be interviewed, _____?

isn't it?

aren't we?

don't they?

did she?

can't you?

shouldn't they?

do they?

didn't he?

are we?

3 How do you say it in English?

Write the sentences in English.

1. Er kann kochen, nicht wahr?

   _____

2. Du magst das Essen in der Schulkantine, richtig?

   _____

3. Ich muss das nicht essen, oder?

   _____

4. Deine Schwester hat noch kein Sushi gegessen, gell?

   _____

5. Ihr dürft gar keine Süßigkeiten essen, nicht wahr?

   _____

Over to you

You have got a new friend from England. You don't know much about his or her eating habits, but you know some facts. He or she will visit you soon. That's why you want to know more. Finish the message and use question tags to ask if what you know is right. There are some ideas in the box.

often eat hot dishes | love sweets | enjoy cooking | be good at baking | can't stand chocolate | ...

Hi, I would like to know more about your eating habits. You like fish and chips, don't you?

_____

_____

_____

_____

Introduction

Hi, this is Jason. I'm reporting live from my hometown. At the moment, I'm standing in the street next to my house. There is a car boot sale and I want to see what is going on there. I can see a woman and her daughter. They are selling snacks and cakes. Another girl is talking to a group of kids. I think they are discussing the price of a pair of sunglasses. Some metres away, an old man is taking out lots of glasses and plates from his car, but his wife isn't setting up the stall. She is talking to a man. He is carrying a big bag and he is wearing a black hat. Now he is buying something from her but he isn't giving her any money. They must be friends. What are you doing right now? Please leave a comment and tell me.

Language Tip

Mit der **Verlaufsform der Gegenwart** (*present progressive*) drückt man aus, was jemand gerade tut oder was gerade passiert. Die Ereignisse sind noch nicht abgeschlossen.

Vergangenheit   *Gegenwart*   *Zukunft*

Die Verlaufsform wird gebildet mit einer Form von *be (am/is/are)* und der **ing-Form des Verbs**.

Aussagesatz:	**I am reporting live.**	**They are selling snacks.**
Verneinung:	**He isn't paying.**	**They aren't eating pizza.**
Fragen:	**What are you doing?**	**Are they eating lunch?**

Grammatikvideo: **WES-149143-006**

Language Detective

a) Highlight all forms of **be** in the **introduction** in blue and all **verbs with -ing** in red.
b) Find the right English expressions for:

1. Sie verkaufen Snacks und Kuchen.   _____

2. Seine Frau baut den Stand nicht auf.   _____

3. Sie redet gerade mit einem Mann.   _____

4. Was macht ihr gerade?   _____

c) Do you speak another language like French or Spanish? Is there a tense which is like the present progressive?
   If yes: What is it called?

   _____

1 At the car boot sale

What are the people at the car boot sale saying? Put the verbs in brackets into the **present progressive**.

1. I _am selling_____ (sell) my old comic books.

2. Look, Gerald _____ (buy) something.

3. Can you smell that? Maggie and John _____ (make) some crêpes at their stall.

4. Ouch. You _____ (stand) on my foot.

5. Where are Adrian and Bella? – They _____ (look) at the video games.

6. Why is Helen not here? – She _____ (help) Dad with the food.

7. Wow, look at Sue. She _____ (wear) a nice dress.

8. A man in a black hat _____ (give) her some money.

9. Oh, there is Brendon. He _____ (walk) towards Mr Tubbs with the phone cases.

2 Questions

What are the people asking? Make the right questions.

1. What – you – sell?   _What are you selling?_____

2. Where – they – go?   _____

3. What – he – look at?   _____

4. his phone – work?   _____

5. Why – you wear – that old dress? _____

6. What – she – cook?   _____

3 No, they aren't!

Complete the short answers of the people at the car boot sale.

1. Are they selling clothes?   No, _they aren't_____ . They are only selling books.

2. Is he buying all her comic books?   Yes, _____ . All of them.

3. Are you drinking my milkshake?   No, _____ . This one is mine.

4. Is she really going home?   Yes, _____ . She has sold everything.

5. Are you waiting for your dad?   No, _____ . He has already gone home.

6. Are they running for the bus?   Yes, _____ .

7. Is that bus going to Camden Market?   No, _____ . It's going to West Ham.

4 How do you say it in English?

You are watching a TV series with your English-speaking friend. Tell her what the teenagers Daniel and Melanie in the series are saying so that she can understand.

1. Daniel: Melanie, was machst du gerade?

   You: _Daniel is asking what Melanie is doing right now._____

   Melanie: Ich suche gerade nach Comicheften auf dem Flohmarkt. Meine Eltern verkaufen hier Getränke.

   You: _____

   _____

2. Daniel: Ich hoffe, die Sonne scheint gerade. Bei uns regnet es.

   You: _____

3. Melanie: Gerade fängt es an zu regnen. Jetzt renne ich in ein Geschäft.

   You: _____

   _____

4. Daniel: Meine Mutter kommt gerade nach Hause.

   You: _____

   Melanie: Alles klar. Lass uns doch später noch mal telefonieren. Ich rufe dich an, wenn ich wieder zuhause

   bin. Schön, dass du angerufen hast.

EXERCISE They are selling snacks.

5 Right now?

What are YOU doing right now? What is happening? Write true sentences
(positive or negative) in the **present progressive**.

1. sell things at a flea market: _I am not selling things at a flea market._

2. have dinner: _____

3. wear shoes: _____

4. ride my bike: _____

5. it – rain: _____

6. the sun – shine: _____

Over to you

Imagine you are at a flea market right now. Write a message to a friend and tell him or her what is happening
there. The words and phrases in the boxes can help you.

| tourists | children | teenagers |
| parents | dogs | police officers | ... |

| buy a book | sell waffles | walk around | look at the items |
| make a selfie | talk to a seller | look for something | ... |

Hi _____. I am at a flea market right now.

_____

_____

_____

_____

_____

_____

_____

_____

Introduction

The Vikings

The Vikings were people who sailed the seas as early as the year 900. The Vikings had ships which were good enough to take them all across the Atlantic Ocean. So it was not Columbus who was the first European to sail to America, but it was the Vikings who arrived in America hundreds of years earlier.

At the same time, they also visited Great Britain. These visits were not very friendly. They burned down villages and took everything. They had weapons which were very strong.

Because of the ships which brought them to places far away, they were also able to sell goods to people in other countries. Their customers were people who lived all over the world.

The Vikings had different gods. For example there was "Thor" who was the god of thunder[1].

Language Tip

Mit Relativsätzen kannst du eine Person oder eine Sache näher beschreiben. Ein Relativsatz beginnt meist mit einem Relativpronomen: **who**, **which** oder **that**.

Dabei verwendest du *who* für **Personen** und *which* für **Dinge**. *That* kannst du sowohl für **Personen** als auch **Dinge** verwenden.

Beispiele: The Vikings were people **who** sailed the seas.
They had weapons **which** were strong.

Grammatikvideo: **WES-149143-007**

Language Detective

a) Highlight all **relative pronouns** in the **introduction**. Use red for **who** and green for **which**.
b) Find the right english expressions for:

1. Es waren die Vikinger, die hunderte Jahre früher in Amerika ankamen.

_____

2. Sie hatten Waffen, die sehr stark waren.

_____

3. Ihre Kunden waren Menschen, die auf der ganzen Welt gelebt haben.

_____

[1]thunder: *Donner*

1 Who or which?

Which relative pronoun do you use for these people or things? Write down **who** or **which**.

1. the boy: _who_   4. many ships: _____   7. something: _____

2. the house: _____   5. people: _____   8. Grandpa: _____

3. the Vikings: _____   6. somebody: _____   9. swords: _____

2 At the Viking festival

What do the people at the Viking festival say? Fill in **who** or **which**.

1. We saw a man _____ looked like an old Viking in his costume.

2. We bought tickets for the show _____ were very expensive.

3. They booked into a hotel _____ was very loud.

4. Can I speak to someone _____ knows the way to the food stalls?

5. The Vikings had ships _____ were very fast and could land on the beach.

6. My uncle is a man _____ is very interested in Viking history and culture.

7. The Vikings used swords and axes, _____ are very dangerous weapons.

8. They wanted to have a look at the stall _____ was selling Viking beards.

3 Who or what is it?

Make correct sentences.

The Vikings were people		grows on your face.
A warrior is someone	who	fights in battles.
A beard is hair	which	you can wear.
A mother is a woman		has got a child.
Costumes are clothes		sailed the seas.

1. _____

2. _____

3. _____

4. _____

5. _____

4 This is an exercise which I like.

Finish the sentences with a **relative clause** that fits.

1. A sword is a weapon *which is very sharp.*

2. Festival staff are people _____

3. Food stalls are the stalls _____

4. A selfie is a photo of you _____

5. A helmet is something _____

6. Sunday is a day _____

7. Hammers are tools _____

Over to you

Imagine you were at a Viking festival. You met lots of people there and you saw lots of things. Write an email to an English-speaking friend and tell him or her about the people and things. Use **relative clauses**. The questions in the box can help you.

- Who did you go there with?
- What could you buy at the stalls?
- What costumes did people wear?
- What did you like the most?
- What food did you eat? What did you drink?
- What was special there?
- Was there a competition / a workshop?
- ...

Hi _____ !

How are you? I want to tell you about the Viking festival which I went to.

Introduction

From	xxxxxxxxxxxxxxxxxxxxxx	✉ @
Reference	Jorvik Viking Festival	

Hi Adrian,

Yesterday my family and I were at the finale of the Jorvik Viking festival. It was great. Lots of people were holding up torches and people were lighting fireworks. My sister Selma was taking lots of photos. She was also wearing a very cool Viking costume, with a long beard and everything. Then the Vikings had a battle. They were fighting with swords and axes. Of course, they weren't really fighting, but it was exciting. We were enjoying the show when my phone suddenly rang. It was Alexa. She said that she was watching the finale live on social media – and that, just for a second, she saw a teenager who looked just like me. And when we were talking, she saw the teenager was talking on his phone, too. So it must have been me! What were you doing yesterday at 8 p.m.? Were you watching the finale, too?
Bye!

Language Tip

Das *past progressive* funktioniert ähnlich wie das *present progressive*, nur dass es Vorgänge in der Vergangenheit (= *past*) beschreibt. Mit dem *past progressive* kannst du beschreiben:

a) was jemand zu einer bestimmten Zeit in der Vergangenheit **gerade tat** oder **was gerade passierte**.

b) **was gerade vor sich ging**, als (plötzlich) etwas anderes geschah bzw. diese Handlung unterbrach.

〰〰〰〰〰 ────┼────·───→

Vergangenheit   Gegenwart   Zukunft

Du bildest das *past progressive* mit *was* oder *were* und dem **Verb in der ing-Form**. Bei Verneinungen hängst du ein *not* hinter *was* oder *were*. Für Fragen stellst du *was* oder *were* an den Satzanfang bzw. hinter das Fragewort.

Aussagesatz:	He was walking home.	We were talking to them.
Verneinung:	He wasn't walking home.	We were not talking to them.
Fragen:	When was he walking home?	Were you talking to them?

🔲 Grammatikvideo: WES-149143-008

Language Detective

a) Highlight all verbs in the past progressive in the **introduction**.

b) Write down one positive statement, one negative statement and one question from the **introduction**:

1. _____ .

2. _____ .

3. _____ ?

1 Was or were?

Who was talking when Talisha got a phone call at the festival? Fill in **was** or **were**.

1. I _____ **talking**.

2. Dad _____ **talking**.

3. Mum _____ **talking**.

4. They _____ **talking**.

5. You _____ **talking**.

6. My friends _____ **talking**.

7. Peter _____ **talking**.

8. We _____ all **talking**.

was / were
+
Verb +-ing

2 What were they doing?

Talisha took some pictures at the Jorvik Viking festival. What were the people doing when Talisha took the pictures? Complete the sentences in the **past progressive**.

1. Emma _____ (bake) Viking bread. She _____

    (mix) flour[1] and water with her hands. People _____ (watch) her.

2. Justin _____ (make) firewood . He _____

    (use) a hammer as a tool. He _____ (explain) to the visitors what he

    _____ (do).

3. Sam _____ (build) a boat. His sister _____

    (help) him. She _____ (stand) in the background when I took the picture.

    Sam _____ (work) the wood with his tools.

4. The actor _____ (pose) for Talisha's picture. He _____

    (wear) an expensive warrior costume and he _____ (carry) a sword.

5. The warriors _____ (train) for the battle scene at the finale.

    They _____ (hold) swords and axes. Their coach

    _____ (tell) them what to do.

[1]flour: *Mehl*

EXERCISE We were watching the show.

3 She wasn't …

Write sentences about what Talisha wasn't doing during the finale of the Jorvik Viking festival.

1. wear a costume   Talisha wasn't wearing a costume.

2. light fireworks   _____

3. film a video   _____

4. eat waffles   _____

5. shop at the stalls   _____

6. put away her mobile phone   _____

4 What were you doing?

a) What questions did the people ask Talisha when she told them about the festival? Make the right questions.

1. What – you – do – when your mobile phone rang?

_____

2. it – rain?

_____

3. Why – your mum – wear a beard?

_____

4. Which weapons – the Vikings – use – during the battle scene?

_____

5. you – take lots of pictures?

_____

b) What questions would YOU ask Talisha about the festival? Write four more questions in the **past progressive**.

1. _____

2. _____

3. _____

4. _____

5 How do you say it in English?

Write the sentences in English.

1. Sie sahen sich gerade die Parade im Fernsehen an.

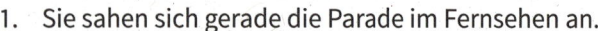

They were watching the parade on television.

2. Die Wikinger in der Show trugen alle lange Bärte.

3. Sie bezahlte gerade die Pommes als ihr Handy klingelte.

4. Ich suchte gerade einen Mülleimer als ich John sah.

5. John telefonierte gerade, aber dann sah er mich.

Over to you

Imagine you are at a parade at a street festival. Write an email to an English-speaking friend and tell him or her what was happening. Use the **simple past** and **past progressive**. The ideas in the boxes can help you.

| visitors | friends | singer | seller | festival staff |
| stall | stage | competition | talent show | concert | …

| watch | buy | eat | make a phone call | take pictures |
| listen to the music | film a video | talk to somebody | …

Introduction

Dear readers,
You all know me by the name of Friday, but that's not my real name. Robinson Crusoe called me Friday because he found me on a Friday. He didn't really find me, but he saw that I was in trouble with some really horrible people who wanted to kill and eat me. So, what did he do? Well, he fired his gun and the cannibals ran away. I wanted to say thank you, but Rob didn't understand me. Of course not, because we both spoke different languages. So, I started to learn English (because I thought my language was too difficult for him and I wanted to be nice) and we became quite good friends. The funny thing was that first, Rob believed that he was so much cleverer than me. So, he thought that he was my teacher, and I was his student. Well, Rob found out very soon that I was able to show him quite a few things, too. I'll tell you more about that in my next article.

Language Tip

Das *simple past* verwendest du, um über Dinge zu sprechen, die in der Vergangenheit passiert und vorbei sind.

Vergangenheit   Gegenwart   Zukunft

Die meisten Verben sind **regelmäßig**. Um die Vergangenheitsform zu bilden, hängst du ein **-ed** an diese Verben an: like ➜ lik**ed**   walk ➜ walk**ed**
Die **unregelmäßigen Verben** musst du lernen (siehe S. 78-80).

Aussagen:	**He called me Friday.**
Verneinung:	**They didn't get me.**
Fragen:	**Did you go to England?**

Endet das Verb mit einem -e, dann hängst du nur ein **-d** an (z. B. **liked**).
Endet das Verb auf einen kurzen betonten Vokal und einen Konsonanten, dann wird der Konsonant verdoppelt (z. B. **stopped**).

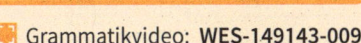 Grammatikvideo: WES-149143-009

Language Detective

a) Highlight all **verbs** in the **introduction** that are in the **simple past**.
b) Find the **simple past** forms of these verbs:

1. find _____

2. see _____

3. do _____

4. fire _____

5. speak _____

6. become _____

7. is _____

8. am able to _____

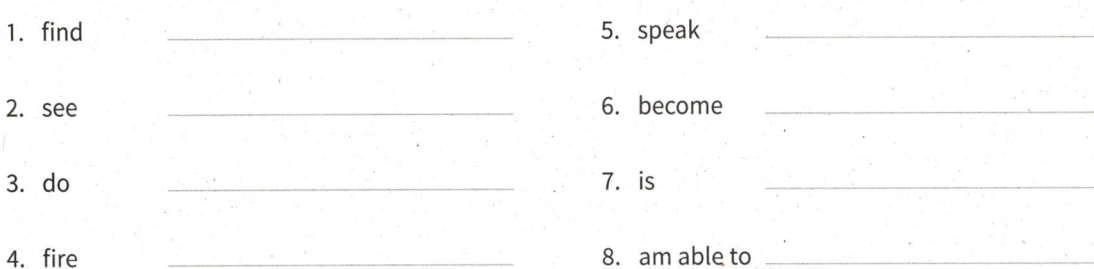

1 do - did

Fill in the table.

infinitive	simple past	infinitive	simple past
do	did	tell	
go		sell	
get		take	
have		stand	
stay		see	
open		be	
put		know	
leave		eat	
make		listen	
find		lose	
swim		cross	
hear		hit	
think		buy	

2 How a dolphin saved me

Read the blog entry. Fill in the simple past forms of the verbs in the box.

be (x 2) | swim | can | have | touch | fall | see (x 2) | hit | think | help | say

Fifty years ago my friends and I _____ on a boat trip in the Caribbean, when in the

middle of the night a storm _____ . I _____ overboard and nobody

_____ me. But I _____ lucky, because I _____ my

life jacket on and I am a good swimmer, too. So I _____ to the beach as quickly as I

_____ . Then something _____ my leg. What a scary situation.

First I _____ it was a shark, but then I _____ that two dolphins were

swimming next to me. One of them _____ me to get to the beach.

I _____ : "Thank you so much for rescuing me."

3 My friend Friday and I

What did Robinson Crusoe tell his friends? Make the correct negative sentences.

1. Friday – not speak – English. Friday didn't speak English.

2. At first – I – not understand him. _____

3. He – not be able to write. _____

4. I – not know – how to fish. _____

5. We – not have – any problems. _____

6. The cannibals – not find us again. _____

7. I – not be – afraid. _____

4 What was the question?

What did a reporter ask Robinson when he was back in England? Write down the questions for the answers.

1. Did you meet anybody on the island? _____

   - Yes, I did. After some years I met a man on the island.

2. _____

   - I am not sure if he had a name, but I called him "Friday".

3. _____

   - I called him Friday because we met on a Friday.

4. _____

   - He taught me how to catch fish.

5. _____

   - The ship brought us to England.

6. _____

   - Yes, he did. Friday came with me.

7. _____

   - No, we didn't. When we first arrived here we didn't miss anything about the island.

5 How do you say it in English?

Write the right English sentences.

1. Wir waren auf einer einsamen Insel.

   _____

2. Wir hatten ein Problem, weil wir keine Zahnbürsten dabei hatten.

   _____

3. Wir haben Blätter verwendet, um Wasser zu sammeln.

   _____

4. Alle dachten, dass wir ein Messer bräuchten.

   _____

5. Wir vermissten unsere Freunde sehr, doch es war auch ein großes Abenteuer.

   _____

Over to you

Imagine you were stranded on a desert island. Now you are back at home. Write a blog entry about your time on the island. Use the **simple past**. The questions in the box can help you.

- How did you get to the island?
- Who was there with you?
- How did you get food/water?
- Did something bad happen?
- How did you get home?
- ...

Hi guys!

Introduction

Some of you asked me if I could answer some questions about what you need if you want to survive alone on an island. Here is what I think: First, you need to find some water – and something to keep the water in. So, a bottle would be very useful because you can take it to any place you like. Second, a knife would be useful, because you need something to cut plants or maybe even kill some animals for food. Then you need something to make fire with. A box of matches would be great. But if you don't have any matches, then you'll need to learn how to make fire with something else, for example with stones. Can you use any kind of stones? No, you need the right stones. Is there anything else you need? You need some safe place where you can sleep and relax. So, you need to find something to build your home with.

Language Tip

Mit *some* und *any* werden Mengen bezeichnet wie „etwas", „einige" oder „viele", während **not ... any** mit „kein" oder „keine" übersetzt werden kann. Bei **bejahten Aussagesätzen** verwendest du also *some*, bei **Verneinungen und Fragen** verwendest du *any*. Nach denselben Regeln benutzt du auch *something* und *anything*. Eine Ausnahme gibt es: Wenn du jemanden höflich um etwas bittest, oder ihm etwas anbietest, verwendest du in Fragen auch *some* bzw. *something*.

Aussagesatz:	**We need some water.**	**We need something to drink.**
Verneinung:	**I can't find any water.**	**There isn't anything on this island.**
Fragen:	**Do we have any fruit?**	**Is there anything else?**
	Would you like some mangos?	**Can I have something to drink, please?**

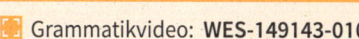 Grammatikvideo: WES-149143-010

Language Detective

a) Highlight **some** and **something** in the **introduction** in green, **any** and **anything** in red.
b) Find the english expressions for:

1. Als Erstes musst du etwas Wasser finden. _____

2. Du brauchst etwas, um Pflanzen zu schneiden. _____

3. Wenn du keine Streichhölzer hast, ... _____

4. Gibt es noch etwas, das du brauchst? _____

5. Du brauchst etwas, um ein Zuhause zu bauen. _____

1 What do you need on a desert island?

Complete the sentences with **something** and **anything**.

1. First, you need _____ to drink. This can be water or fruit juice.

2. If you don't have _____ to eat, you have to find fruit or hunt animals on the island.

3. If you have fire, you can cook animals and heat up water to clean it. Don't eat or drink

   _____ that is dirty!

4. You also need _____ to clean your teeth with so that they don't go bad.

5. On an island, you will find _____ to build a small house with. You need a shelter.

6. You can use wood, for example, and _____ soft and long to put it together so that

   it becomes a small house.

2 Alone on the island

How did Peter survive alone on an island? Read the text and fill in the right words from the box.

some | any | something | anything

Let me tell you _____ something _____ about my biggest

adventure ever. There I was, alone on an island. The good thing was

that I had a knife and _____ matches, but I didn't have

_____ to drink. So I looked around to see if I could find _____

water. First, I couldn't find _____ water. Then I saw _____

coconuts. I opened them with my knife and drank the coconut water. On the second day I was lucky. I found

a little river. I took _____ of the water with me. I could also see _____

fish. I had not eaten _____ that day yet. I tried to catch one of them. It was

very difficult, and I didn't catch _____ at all. I had to practise. I looked for

_____ sticks and I sharpened them with my knife. After two days eating only coconuts

I actually caught a fish. I had to eat it without _____ salt, but it was better than

nothing! Later I also learnt how to collect _____ water with leaves.

3 How do you say it in English?

You are three people on an island. Marcel speaks German, but Tia speaks English.
Help them to understand each other.

1. Marcel: Kannst du Tia bitte mal fragen, ob wir noch etwas zu trinken haben?

    You: _____

2. Tia: We haven't got any coconut water left, but I found some water in leaves earlier. So yes.

    You: _____

3. Marcel: Möchte Tia etwas zu essen? Wir haben noch Fisch und rote Früchte.

    You: _____

4. Tia: Yes, thanks. I am very hungry. Can you tell me something about this island?

    You: _____

5. Marcel: Ich weiß leider nichts über die Insel hier. So etwas Schönes habe ich aber noch nie gesehen.

    You: _____

    _____

Over to you

You are on an island – alone or only with one or two friends. Write a diary entry about a day there. You can
note down the things that are there or aren't there on the island or about things that have happened since you
became stranded there. Use **some**, **any**, **something** and **anything**.

Dear diary,

There is something I need to tell you.

Introduction

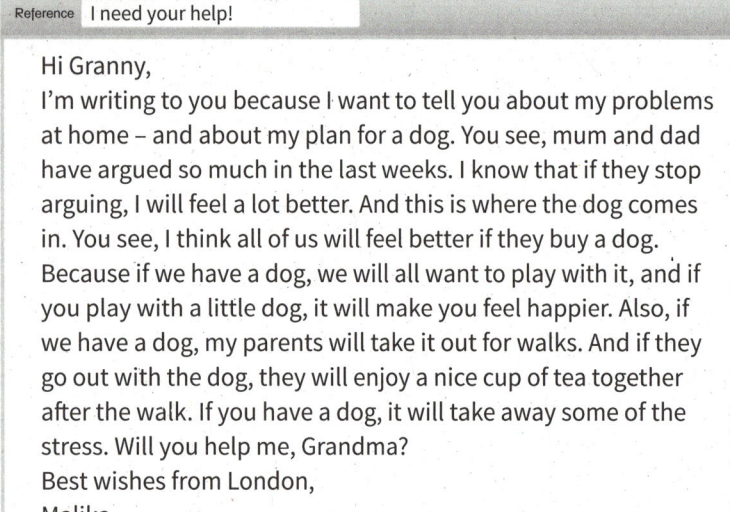

From _____ ✉ @

Reference | I need your help!

Hi Granny,
I'm writing to you because I want to tell you about my problems
at home – and about my plan for a dog. You see, mum and dad
have argued so much in the last weeks. I know that if they stop
arguing, I will feel a lot better. And this is where the dog comes
in. You see, I think all of us will feel better if they buy a dog.
Because if we have a dog, we will all want to play with it, and if
you play with a little dog, it will make you feel happier. Also, if
we have a dog, my parents will take it out for walks. And if they
go out with the dog, they will enjoy a nice cup of tea together
after the walk. If you have a dog, it will take away some of the
stress. Will you help me, Grandma?
Best wishes from London,
Malika

Language Tip

Wenn du sagen möchtest, was **unter bestimmten Bedingungen** geschehen wird oder geschehen kann, benutzt
du einen **Bedingungssatz** (*If-clause*). Der If-Satz kann dabei an erster oder zweiter Stelle stehen. Wenn der If-Satz
zuerst kommt, setzt du ein Komma.

Bedingung:	Folge:		Folge:	Bedingung:
If we **have** a dog,	we **will play** with it.		I **will feel** better	if they **stop** arguing.
simple present	will-future		will-future	simple present

 Grammatikvideo: **WES-149143-011**

Language Detective

a) Highlight all **conditions** *(Bedingungen)* in the **introduction** in red and
   all **results** *(Folgen)* in blue.
b) Complete the sentences with the conditions from the **introduction**.

1. _____ , I will feel a lot better.

2. All of us will feel better _____ .

3. _____ , this will make you feel happier.

4. _____ , they will enjoy a nice cup of tea together.

c) Explain: why isn't there a comma in sentence 2. ?

1 If it rains ...

Cross out the wrong parts of the sentences.

1. If it **rains / ~~will rain~~** on Sunday, we **will stay / stay** at home.

2. If the weather **is / will be** good, I **will go / go** skateboarding.

3. My dad **makes / will make** breakfast tomorrow if he **gets up / will get up** early.

4. I **will do / do** my homework later if I **will go / go** skateboarding now.

5. If my grandparents **visit / will visit** us, it **is / will be** lots of fun.

6. If we **play / will play** board games together, my grandma **wins / will win**.

7. If my bike **is / will be** broken, I **take / will take** the bus to school.

2 Solving problems

Write If-sentences.

1 my dad – need help with making pancakes ⇒	I – show him how to do it
2 the weather – be bad ⇒	Peter – stay inside and play games
3 I – come home very late ⇒	I – get into trouble with my parents
4 our dog Bello – want to go outside ⇒	we – take him for a walk
5 my sister – can't do her homework ⇒	my mum – help her
6 my mum – tell me to tidy up ⇒	I – tell her I have to do my homework

1. *If my dad needs help with making pancakes, I will show him how to do it.*

2. _____

3. _____

4. _____

5. _____

6. _____

3 More problems

Make sentences with **if** in the middle.

I – talk to you on the phone		you – not do your English homework.
I – be able to do the school project		you – help me.
You – get a bad cold	if	you – not come to the match.
Your teammates – understand		you – bring cake to school.
Everybody – be happy		you – not be able to come to my house.
You – be in trouble with Mr. Jenkins		you – not wear a warm jacket.

1. I will talk to you on the phone if you aren't able to come to my house.

2.

3.

4.

5.

6.

4 Sentence chain

a) Use the next sentence to complete your sentence.

1. If you don't have any breakfast …
2. If you are hungry at school …
3. If you aren't able to concentrate on your schoolwork…
4. If your schoolwork isn't so good…
5. If you feel stressed out…
6. you be unhappy.

1. If you don't have any breakfast, you will be hungry at school.

2. If you are hungry at school,

3.

4.

5.

b) Make one more sentence with your own idea.

5 How do you say it in English?

Write the sentences in English.

1. Wenn er seine Hausaufgaben nicht macht, wird er Ärger bekommen.

_____

2. Wenn ihr nicht aufhört zu streiten, werde ich nach Hause gehen.

_____

3. Bekomme ich etwas Taschengeld, wenn ich das Auto sauber mache?

_____

4. Wenn ich den Film nicht anschauen darf, dann werde ich Musik hören.

_____

5. Wenn wir heute ins Kino gehen, sehen wir uns James Bond an.

_____

Over to you

Write an email to an English-speaking friend. Tell him or her about a problem you have and say what you will do if certain things happen. The situations in the box can help you.

- not get any pocket money
- miss your friends
- feel sad because ...
- not get invited to a party
- forget your homework
- move away
- feel extremely tired
- weather is bad all the time
- get bad marks at school

Hi _____!

_____

_____

_____

_____

_____

_____

Introduction

Yesterday Bernice looked at herself in the mirror. She thought she would have to put on some make-up to make herself look more beautiful, but then she talked to her grandma via videochat. Her grandma told her: "Now, Bernice, you don't need to feel bad about yourself. Sometimes people look at themselves and don't like what they see, but I can tell you, you look just fine. It's not so important what people look like, but what they do and if they are nice to others." Then Bernice went online and saw a hashtag #ourselves. People posted pictures of themselves without make-up. They were all beautiful. There was one old man who looked just like her grandpa. He took the picture himself with his phone. He wrote: "I wasn't always happy with myself, but I am now."

"I wasn't always happy with myself, but I am now."

Language Tip

Reflexivpronomen beziehen sich auf das Subjekt in einem Satz (wer oder was?). Sie werden im Englischen im **-self (Einzahl)** oder **-selves (Mehrzahl)** gebildet. Im Englischen werden Reflexivpronomen auch benutzt, um ein Nomen oder Pronomen besonders zu betonen. Sie bedeuten dann „selbst" oder „selber".

Beispiele: She saw **herself** in a mirror.
                 They saw **themselves** in a mirror.

Language Detective

a) Highlight all **reflexive pronouns** in the **introduction**.
b) Complete the table. All missing reflexive pronouns are in the **introduction**.

personal pronoun	reflexive pronoun
I	
you	
he	
she	
it	itself
we	
you	yourselves
they	

1 I like myself.

Which **reflexive pronoun** do you use? Write them on the lines.

1. I like _____ .

2. Justin, you like _____ .

3. My sister likes _____ .

4. My sister and I like _____ .

5. My dad likes _____ .

6. You two like _____ .

7. Bill and Bob like _____ .

8. Jenny and Mia like _____ .

9. We like _____ .

10. The robot likes _____ .

2 Be careful about what you post!

Fill in the right **reflexive pronouns**.

Hi everyone!

I am Brenda. I would like to give you some tips about how to stay safe online and also tell you something about how I made a big mistake _____ . Here is the thing: Don't post any embarrassing photos of _____ online. Never!

Lisa, one of my friends, recently posted a picture of _____ in funny clothes and she was very sad about all the bad comments she got. When Peter repaired his bike _____ , he posted a short video about how he did it. It was just a normal vlog, but he still got weird comments.

We all post things on social media and some time later we are very unhappy that there are photos of _____ online. I mean, the internet doesn't forget! Actually, I put a really stupid photo of _____ online once. My mum saw it and was very angry at _____ because she was the one who allowed me to use social media. People can enjoy _____ on social media. We all just have to be careful about what we want to share with the world. One last thing: Don't ever feel bad about _____ because of pictures you saw online. Mostly, people use filters and are not just _____ .

3   How do you say it in German?

Write the right German sentences.

1. Oh no! I have cut myself.

_____

2. The cat often washes itself.

_____

3. We will go to the party and enjoy ourselves!

_____

4. Jane is looking at herself in a mirror.

_____

5. Don't feel bad about yourself because of pictures you see online.

_____

Over to you

Your parents are away for the weekend. Now you want to write a short message to an English-speaking friend and tell him or her five things you, your brothers and sisters have done yourselves while your parents are away. You can use the ideas in the box.

repair a bike | make waffles | enjoy myself | finish a school project | clean the house | make a cake | ...

Hi _____ ! Guess what: my parents are away for the

weekend!

_____

_____

_____

_____

_____

Introduction

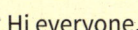

Hi everyone,
Let me tell you about my favourite invention ever. It's my beloved
teddy bear. Did you know that the first teddy was made in 1902?
Well, my teddy isn't quite that old. But Charles, that's what he
is called, is almost a hundred years old. I think he was bought
in the 1920s and given to Annie, my great-great grandmother,
as a birthday present. In 1954 something terrible happened to
him: his eyes were taken out. We don't really know who did it.
Well, from then on Charles was taken good care of. But one day,
another bad thing happened to Charles: he was taken away by
our dog, and it took three days until he was found again. Thank
goodness he was not broken.
What is your favourite invention? I think lots of great things are
invented nowadays. I am looking forward to the future!

Language Tip

Sätze im Aktiv sagen uns, wer oder was handelt. Wenn es aber nicht wichtig oder klar ist, wer etwas tut oder
getan hat, kannst du das **Passiv** verwenden.

Das Passiv bildest du mit einer **Form von** *be* + **Partizip Perfekt (3. Form des Verbes)**. Das heißt, du setzt
praktisch immer die Form von **be** in die richtige Zeit und setzt dahinter das Partizip Perfekt des Verbs.

Beispiele:

simple present

English **is spoken** all over the world.
Teddys **are bought** by adults.

simple past

Latin **was spoken** in Athens.
Teddys **were invented** a long time ago.

Grammatikvideo: WES-149143-013

Language Detective

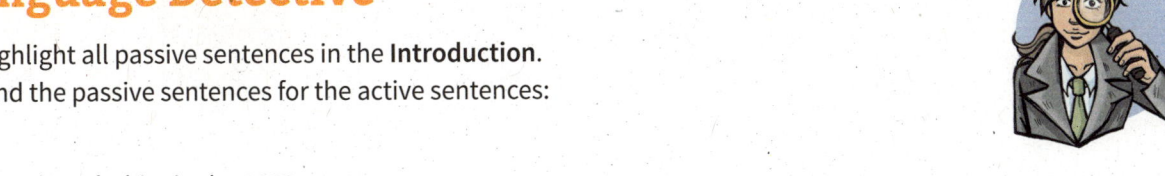

a) Highlight all passive sentences in the **Introduction**.
b) Find the passive sentences for the active sentences:

1. They bought him in the 1920s. _____

2. Someone took out his eyes. _____

3. People took good care of Charles. _____

4. They found him again. _____

5. They invent lots of great things. _____

1 Past participle

Fill in the table with the right verb forms.

infinitive	past participle
break	broken
catch	
cut	
find	
forget	

infinitive	past participle
keep	
know	
pay	
show	
take	

2 Facts about inventions

Fill the gaps with the past participle of the verbs in the box to make the **passive** of the **simple present**.

sell | find | use | eat | ~~make~~ | put

1. Windows **are** ____made____ of glass.

2. Stamps **are** _____ online.

3. The letter **is** _____ into the mailbox.

4. Computers **are** _____ everywhere.

5. Microwaves **are** _____ in many kitchens.

6. Chocolate chip cookies **are** _____ all over the world.

3 Inventions at home

Fill the gaps with the verbs in the **passive** of the **simple past**.

1. The television ____was bought____ (buy) last year.

2. My bike _____ (steal) yesterday.

3. Our grandpa's old car _____ (put) into a museum.

4. All these apps _____ (upload) in the past few days.

5. In 1876 the telephone _____ (invent).

6. My T-shirt _____ (make) in Asia.

7. The houses here _____ (build) in the 1990s.

4 Getting the facts right

Mia read some wrong facts on the internet. She needs to correct them. Write sentences and use the right tense.

1. The light bulb was not invented by Shakespeare.

   It / invent / by Thomas Edison.

   _____

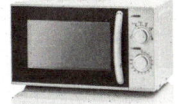

2. Microwaves are not used to heat rooms.

   They / use / to heat up food.

   _____

3. Children are not brought to school by plane.

   They / bring to school / by car.

   _____

4. Stamps are not put on cars.

   They / put on / letters.

   _____

5 It was written by ...

Make sentences in the passive of the **simple past** or **simple present**. Use a suitable verb.

1. Harry Potter / by J.K. Rowling:

   Harry Potter was written by J.K. Rowling.

2. One of the first computers / "Baby":

   _____

3. More than 120 million smartphones / in 2007:

   _____

4. The guitar / all over the world:

   _____

5. Sushi / not only in Japan:

   _____

6 From active to passive

Put the active sentences into the passive. Use the same tense.

1. They make this cup from paper.

This cup is made from paper.

2. Someone sent the first text message in 1992.

3. They play video games all over the world.

4. People usually eat muesli with milk.

5. Sir Arthur Conan Doyle wrote the Sherlock Holmes stories more than a hundred years ago.

Over to you

Write a short blog entry about your favourite invention. You can use the information from your textbook and the questions in the box. Use sentences in the passive.

- How was it invented?
- What is it used for?
- Who was it invented by?
- Where was it invented?
- When was it invented?
- What is it made of?
- Why is it liked by many people?
- How do you use it?
- ...

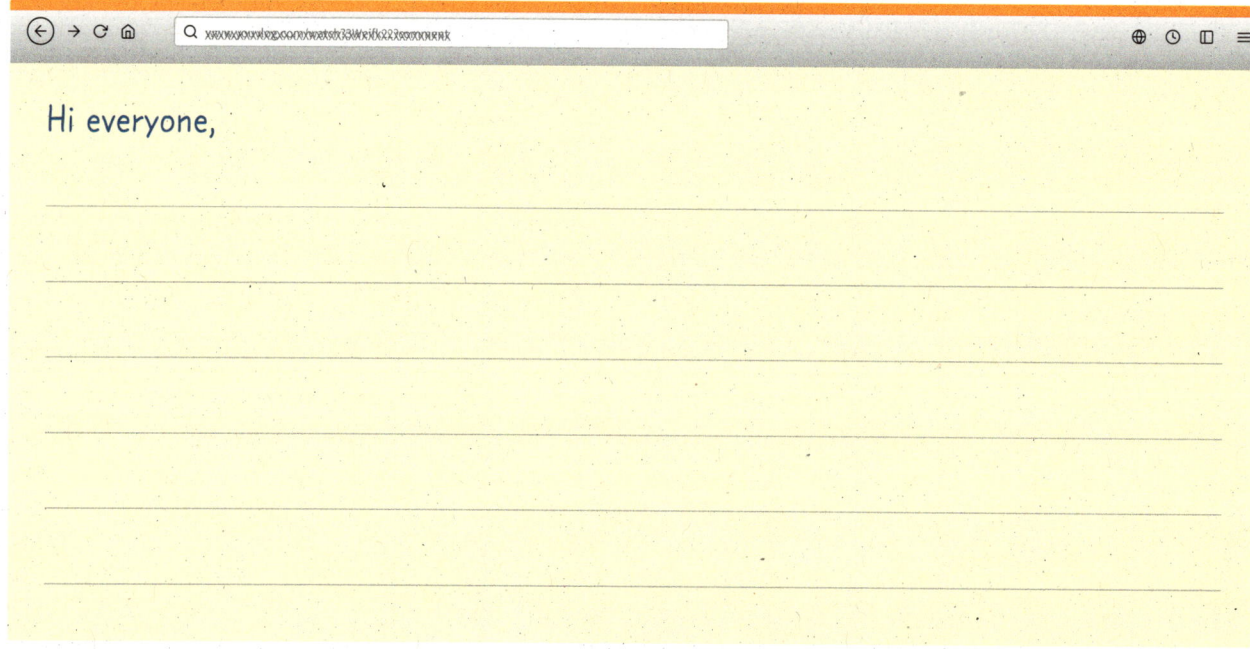

Hi everyone,

Introduction

Layla:	Hi Andrew. Nice to see you. Where are you going?
Andrew:	I'm going to Cardiff. My train left five minutes ago, but there is another one coming in thirty minutes.
Layla:	My sister went to Cardiff last year and she didn't really like it there. She said it was very, very rainy. I have never been to Cardiff. Maybe I will go in August, but I haven't decided yet.
Andrew:	I think Cardiff is great. I went there last year. My family and I did a lot of interesting things. Have you ever heard about the dolphins and whales you can see there?
Layla:	Yes, I have. My brother has always been very interested in sea animals. Did you go to the castle last year? I heard it is very beautiful.
Andrew:	Sadly I have never been to the castle, but I want to go there next week. I can send you some pictures.
Layla:	Lovely. That would be great.

Language Tip

Das *simple past* verwendest du, wenn du über Ereignisse redest, die bereits abgeschlossen sind. Beim *present perfect* ist die Handlung noch nicht abgeschlossen oder sie hat eine Bedeutung für die Gegenwart.

simple past

Vergangenheit　　Gegenwart　　Zukunft

present perfect

Vergangenheit　　Gegenwart　　Zukunft

Signalwörter:
yesterday, last Monday, last week, last year, two days ago, three weeks ago, in 1989

Signalwörter:
already, just, never, ever, not ... yet

Grammatikvideo: **WES-149143-014**

Language Detective

a) Highlight all verbs in the **simple past** in the introduction in green and all verbs in the **present perfect** in blue.

b) Write down how to form sentences in the tenses:

simple past

Verb + - _____

oder irreguläres Verb
(in der 2. Form/simple past)

present perfect

_____ / _____ + Verb + - _____

oder irreguläres Verb
(in der 3. Form/past
participle)

1 Signal words

Fill the table with the signal words.

> yesterday | last week | already | not … yet | two years ago | never | last winter | in 1995

simple past	present perfect

2 At the station

What mistakes do the tourists at the station make? Cross out the wrong parts and correct them on the lines.

Oh no! I ~~didn't buy~~ a ticket yet. The train leaves in a few minutes.

haven't bought

Why haven't you been on the train ten minutes ago?

_____

The train did already leave. We will have to wait for the next one.

_____

I have gone to Wales last year.

_____

I did never hear this song before. It's great!

_____

I am so bored. The train didn't arrive yet.

_____

EXERCISE Have been or was?

3 Holidays

What do the teenagers say? Fill the gaps with the verbs in the right tense: **simple past** or **present perfect**.

Oliver: Hi Brendon! My name is Oliver. Nice to meet you. That is a picture of Edinburgh, isn't it?

_____ (you / ever / be) to Scotland?

Brendon: Yes, I _____ . I _____ (go) there last year with my family.

We _____ (visit) Edinburgh and _____ (have) lots of fun.

Oliver: _____ (you / see) Edinburgh Castle, too?

Brendon: Yes, we _____ . We _____ (find) it really interesting.

Last year we only _____ (stay) in Edinburgh. I _____

_____ (never / be) to the Highlands. That's still on my list.

_____ (I / never / see) any of the Lochs.

Oliver: Well, will you go back to Scotland soon?

Brendon: I don't know. My parents said because we _____ (already / be) to Scotland,

we should go somewhere else this year like Italy or Germany. We _____

_____ (not decide yet).

Oliver: Germany sounds nice. I _____ (never / be) there.

4 Which one is it?

Simple past or **present perfect**? Write the sentences in the right tense.

1. I – already – buy – the tickets.   I have already bought the tickets.

2. I – go – to Wales – last year.   _____

3. The train – arrive – an hour ago.   _____

4. Yesterday – I – lose – my phone.   _____

5. You – ever – milk – a highland cow?   _____

6. You – go – to the cinema – last week?   _____

7. When – you – go – to Spain?   _____

5 How do you say it in English?

Write the English sentences. Be careful: sometimes you use different tenses in English than in German!

1. Warst du schon mal in Brighton?

    _____

2. Wo warst du letztes Jahr?

    _____

3. Ist der Zug schon abgefahren?

    _____

4. Ich habe noch keine Flasche Wasser gekauft.

    _____

5. Hat er den Zug gestern verpasst?

    _____

Over to you

Write a blog entry about holidays. Tell the readers what you have never or already done, where you went and when you went there. Write at least 8 sentences. The ideas in the box can help you.

> go to Spain / France / ... | sleep for twelve hours | fly on a plane | do a road trip | hike in the mountains |
> visit grandparents abroad | go bungee jumping | watch dolphins | take selfies in front of a sight | ...

Hey everyone!

Introduction

Last year I went to Scotland for the first time. The weather was "typically" Scottish. It rained heavily and it was cold. When my family and I took a trip to Loch Ness, I secretly hoped that we would see the famous monster. It was cloudy and dark when we arrived at the Loch. And then everything happened so quickly. Something moved in the water. I watched it carefully. It looked like it had a long neck. "What is that?" my brother asked scaredly. "I have no idea. It's moving so fast," my dad answered loudly. "Let's get out of here - now." Mum turned the car around and we drove off as quickly as we could. Well, we never really found out what we saw, but I believe it was Nessie. My dad always tells people excitedly about our time in Scotland and about the trip to Loch Ness. People always tell him laughingly: "Don't be silly, you know Nessie doesn't exist!"

Language Tip

Wenn du eine Sache oder eine Person – also ein Substantiv – beschreiben willst, benutzt du ein Adjektiv.

a <u>big</u> woman   a <u>clever</u> girl   an <u>easy</u> test

Aber wenn aber eine **Tätigkeit**, also ein Verb beschreiben willst bzw. **wie jemand etwas tut**, oder **wie etwas geschieht**, dann benutzt du ein **Adverb**. Adverbien der Art und Weise bildest du, indem du an das Adjektiv ein **-ly** hängst.

slow – **slowly** , **quick** – **quickly**

> Bei manchen Adverbien ändert sich die Schreibweise, wenn -ly angehängt wird.
> **-y** wird zu **-ily,** z. B. **happy** – **happily**
> **-le** wird zu **-ly**, z. B. **terrible** – **terribly**

<u>Achtung Ausnahmen:</u>
good – **well**, **fast** – **fast**, **hard** – **hard** (hardly heißt kaum!)

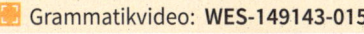 Grammatikvideo: **WES-149143-015**

Language Detective

a) Highlight all **adverbs** in the **introduction**.
b) Find the english expressions for:

1. Ich hoffte insgeheim, dass wir das berühmte Monster sehen werden.

_____

2. Alles geschah dann so plötzlich.

_____

3. Wir fuhren so schnell wir konnten davon.

_____

1 Holidays in Scotland

Look at the pictures from the Miller family's trip to Scotland. Fill in the right adverbs from the box.

beautifully | fast | hungrily | hard | angrily | cutely

1. Nessie can swim very _____ .

2. The man was shouting at them _____ .

3. Josh smiled _____ for the picture.

4. The men were pulling the rope _____ .

5. The pony ate the grass _____ .

6. He played the bagpipes _____ .

2 Adverbs

Fill in the table.

adjective	adverb
beautiful	beautifully
terrible	
bad	
loud	
slow	

adjective	adverb
good	
short	
happy	
easy	
hard	

3 Adjective or adverb?

Read Ada Miller's diary entry. Cross out the wrong words.

Dear diary,

When we arrived in Scotland, it was raining **heavy / heavily**. Our hotel is very **nice / nicely**. On our first day

here we slept very **good / well**. My parents wanted to visit Urquart Castle. They were talking about it

excited / excitedly. I wasn't very **excited / excitedly**, because I don't really like old castles. I think they are

boring / boringly. On our trip there the sun was shining **bright / brightly**. Then we drove past a

beautiful / beautifully lake. It was the **famous / famously** Loch Ness. The water sparkled **beautiful /**

beautifully in the sun. My brother Josh and I **secret / secretly** hoped to see the monster. "There it is!" Josh

said **loud / loudly**. The was no monster, of course. My brother just thought it was **funny / funnily**.

4 How do you say it in English?

Write the sentences in English.

1. Er ging schnell zurück ins Hotel.

_____

2. Sie sprach langsam und sehr leise.

_____

3. Die drei Hunde bellten ziemlich laut.

_____

4. Es regnete stark.

_____

5. Der Fisch verschwand schnell wieder.

_____

Over to you

Write a short story about a trip to Loch Ness. Use adjectives and adverbs to make your text sound more exciting.
The questions in the box can help you.

- What was the weather like?
- How did you get there?
- Who came with you?

- What did you see and do there?
- Did something strange happen?
- Was it exciting / boring / ...?

- How did you do the things?
- How did things happen?
- ...

_____

_____

_____

_____

_____

_____

_____

_____

_____

_____

Language Detective

1. the fastest runner at our school
2. as old as we are
3. more interesting things than running

1 Records

1. taller 2. the fastest 3. slower 4. heavier 5. the most difficult 6. more famous 7. the fittest

2 Let's compare!

a) 1. heavier than 2. fitter than 3. easier than 4. more dangerous than 5. more successful than 6. more famous than 7. more, than

b) 1. Football is more interesting than tennis. / Tennis is more interesting than football.
2. PE lessons are better than maths lessons. / Maths lessons are better than PE lessons.
3. Ice hockey is more difficult than hockey. / Hockey is more difficult than ice hockey.

3 Bigger and better

1. faster, the fastest 2. most exciting, more exciting 3. the most successful 4. more dangerous 5. the worst, worse

4 Bernie and Sandy

2. Sandy is taller than Bernie. / Bernie is smaller than Sandy.
3. Sandy is better at school than Bernie. / Bernie is worse at school than Sandy.
4. Sandy is fitter than Bernie.
5. Sandy is a faster swimmer than Bernie. / Bernie is a slower swimmer than Sandy.
6. Sandy does more sports than Bernie.

5 How do you say it in English?

1. Rugby is more dangerous than swimming.
2. Can you hold your breath for more than two minutes?
3. Cycling is not as boring as walking.
4. Where is the next skatepark?
5. He is the most successful German football player.

Over to you (Beispieltext)

Hi guys! Today I am going to write about sports. First of all, I think the best sport is tennis. It is better than sports team sports (like rugby or football). It is usually just one person against another and that makes it one of the most difficult sports that exists. Tennis is also better than dancing, because both men and women can play, and both their games are watched a lot. Not like dancing, where women are more popular than men. Or football where people watch the men more than the women. Some of the most successful tennis players are women, like Serena and Venus Williams or Angelique Kerber.

Language Detective

1. I am not allowed to drink any cola at her house.
2. I mustn't bring any of those energy drinks.
3. I also can't eat fast food.

1 Can or can't?

I'm Sue Anne – a health specialist. I **can** give you some tips about healthy food and I **can** help you if you have a problem! One question many people ask me: **Can't** I eat fast food at all? Well, you **can** eat a burger from time to time, but you **can't** eat too many burgers if you want to stay healthy. Water is really good for you. You **can** drink it every day and as much as you want. You **can't** drink too much fruit juice. There **can** be lots of sugar in it. You **can** make a food diary and then we **can** talk a little more about your eating habits. If you want to know more, you **can** book an online course or a counselling session via telephone. Looking forward to meeting you!

2 Mum …

Mum: You <u>shouldn't</u> put so much sugar into your tea.

Yusuf: Mum, you <u>don't have to</u> tell me what to do.
Why don't you sit next to me and then we <u>can</u> finish eating our toast.

Mum: I think you <u>should</u> brush them more often.

Yusuf: Do I really <u>have to</u> to eat all the vegetables at dinner today?

Mum: I think you <u>should</u> eat them.
Please listen, you <u>must</u> take all your medicine today. It <u>can</u> be very dangerous if you don't.
You <u>can't</u> be late for school today!

3 What are they allowed to do?

1. Ben is not allowed to eat sweets before dinner
2. Pets are not allowed in the shop.
3. Gina's friends are allowed to come to the house.
4. They are allowed (to drink) some coke, but only one can.
5. Jasmine is not allowed to play music after ten o'clock.
6. They are allowed to use mobile phones for their presentations.

4 How do you say it in English?

1. You shouldn't eat too much sugar.
2. The dog mustn't eat chocolate. It is bad for him.
3. Are we allowed to eat the cake?
4. We must not drink the milk.
5. You are not allowed to drink coke.

Over to you (Beispieltext)

- You can have porridge for breakfast. It is healthy, and a little bit keeps you feeling full for a long time.
- You should not eat cake very often. It is fine to eat it sometimes, but it has lots of sugar in it.
- You should eat only one sugary thing per day. Eating a bit of sugar is OK, but lots is bad for you.
- You should never eat fast food, because it is very bad for you, and will make your body feel bad too.
- You can put foods in your lunchbox that give you all the vitamins you need. Something sweet, some vegetables, some fruit, and something to keep you full like bread, rice or pasta.

Language Detective

1. Have you ever eaten German food?
2. He hasn't had "Pumpernickel" yet.
3. I have never been to a German city where ...
4. Have you ever tried Sushi?

1 Choose!

1. I have never eaten sushi. 2. They have never tried Haggis. 3. Have you ever baked a cake?
4. She has never been to Italy.

2 Food and drinks

a)

order	ordered		forget	forgot/forgotten		finish	finished
eat	eaten		try	tried		drink	drunk
cut	cut		cook	cooked			

b)
1. have forgotten
2. has cooked
3. have ordered
4. has eaten
5. have tried
6. has cut
7. has drunk
8. has finished

3 Answers

1. I have made some pizza.
2. He has drunk too much coke.
3. Yes, I have not/haven't put meat in it.
4. No, I have not/haven't bought any muesli.
5. No, they have already left.

4 I haven't done it.

1. haven't finished mine yet
2. hasn't enjoyed it
3. have never been to a Greek restaurant
4. have not eaten there yet
5. have never ordered sushi

5 Questions

1. Has she ever tried fish and chips?
2. Has Timmy ever drunk sparkling water?
3. Have you ever made chocolate cookies?
4. Where has he learned to cook this?
5. Why have they not started their dinner?
6. How have you done it?

6 What has happened?

1. The dog has eaten the homework.
2. The mother has cut the cable.
3. The boy has fallen off his skateboard.
4. Someone has drunk the water.

Over to you (Beispieltext)

Hey everyone! Today I am going to talk to you about my food experiences. I have always eaten lunch at school, which I really like, because the food is really nice and healthy too. Where do you eat lunch, on school days? Have you always eaten there? Here are some foods I have never tried: sushi, insects and frog legs. My friend went to France and tried frog legs, but I haven't been able to try them yet. She said they were delicious, but I don't think I believe her. Have you ever tried frog legs? What did you think about them?

Language Detective

1. How many dishes do you have?
2. Sheila can make so many soups.

3. Is the burger too much for a child?
4. Thanks so much!

1 At the restaurant

1. Look at the man over there. How can he eat so **much** / ~~many~~ pizza?
2. How ~~much~~ / **many** bottles of water have you ordered?
3. Wow. There are so ~~much~~ / **many** dishes on the menu.
4. I think they have put too ~~much~~ / **many** eggs in the cake.
5. How **much** / ~~many~~ lemonade did you drink?
6. That dessert is too **much** / ~~many~~ for me.

2 Indian restaurant

Welcome to our restaurant. We offer you a lot of different dishes from all over India. We use a lot of spices to make our food tasty. But at our restaurant, we don't use much salt, because too much salt is not good for you. We can also offer you some vegetarian food if you don't want to eat so much meat. A lot of people have already tasted our food and we have received so many good reviews. Please book a table online because we do not have so many tables. If there are too many people here, we will have to send you away.

3 How do you say it in English?

1. We don't have much food in the fridge.
2. How much butter do we need for the cake?
3. How many apples have you bought?
4. I have eaten too much chocolate.
5. How much is it?

Over to you (Beispieltext)

Hi guys,
I want to talk about the food for our party. We are lots of people so we need lots of food. I already have a lot of food, but we still need much more. I have got lots of bags of crisps, vegetables and fruit, and lots of cookies. I really like those pretzels with chocolate on them, can one of you bring some of those? But do not bring the ones with chocolate and nuts, I do not like nuts, and also some people are allergic to them. We also need sweets, so can someone bring some. I don't know how many bags we need, maybe one bag each. If you bring more than that it will be too much. I hope I haven't asked for too many things, I think that should be enough. See you at the party!

Language Detective

1. That's stupid, isn't it?
2. That sounds great, doesn't it?

3. I don't eat meat, do I?
4. No, you don't.

1 Records

1. There is a cafeteria at the school, ~~is there~~/ **isn't there**?
2. Sweets for breakfast isn't very healthy, **is it** / ~~isn't it~~?
3. The vegetable dishes are quite expensive, ~~are they~~ / **aren't they**?
4. He has eaten a curry before, ~~has he~~ / **hasn't he**?
5. We shouldn't eat so much sugar, **should we** / ~~shouldn't we~~?
6. You can bring your own food to the cafeteria, ~~can you~~/ **can't you**?
7. She didn't eat the meat, **did she** / ~~didn't she~~?
8. They have never been to our cafeteria, **have they** / ~~haven't they~~?

2 Let's compare!

1. isn't it 2. can't you 3. don't they 4. aren't we 5. are we 6. shouldn't they 7. do they 8. didn't he 9. did she

3 How do you say it in English?

1. He can cook, can't he?
2. You like the food in the school canteen, don't you?
3. I don't need to eat that, do I?
4. Your sister hasn't eaten sushi yet, has she?
5. You are not allowed to eat sweets, are you?

Over to you (Beispieltext)

Hi, I would like to know more about your eating habits. You like fish and chips, don't you? I think you probably do, because it is very popular in England, isn't it? You are good at baking, aren't you? I was thinking we could do some baking together one afternoon while you are here, would you like that? Also you like chocolate, don't you? Because chocolate cake is my favourite flavour of cake, so we can make that, can't we? And for dinner, what sort of foods do you like, you often eat hot dishes, don't you? Does that mean you would like chicken curry? That is one of our favourite dishes to eat for dinner, you would be alright with that wouldn't you? Looking forward to reading your answers, Bye!

Language Detective

1. They are selling snacks and cakes.
2. His wife isn't setting up the stall.

3. She is talking to a man.
4. What are you doing right now?

Beispiel: Spanish- Gerundio phrase, el presente progresivo (estar+ ando/iendo)

1 At the car boot sale

1. am selling
2. is buying
3. are making

4. are standing
5. are looking
6. is helping

7. is wearing
8. is giving
9. is walking

2 Questions

1. What are you selling?
2. Where are they going?
3. What is he looking at?

4. Is his phone working?
5. Why are you wearing that old dress?
6. What is she cooking?

3 No, they aren't!

1. No, they aren't.
2. Yes, he is.
3. No, I'm not.

4. Yes, she is.
5. No, I'm not.
6. Yes, they are.

7. No, it's not.

4 How do you say it in English?

1. Melanie is looking for comic books at the flea market. Her parents are selling drinks there.
2. Daniel hopes the sun is shining because it is raining where he is.
3. For Melanie it is starting to rain, she is running into a shop.
4. Daniel's mother is coming home.

5 Right now?

1. I am not selling things at a flea market.
2. I am not having dinner/I am having dinner.
3. I am not wearing shoes/I am wearing shoes.
4. I am riding my bike/I am not riding my bike.
5. It is raining/it is not raining.
6. The sun is shining/the sun is not shining.

Over to you (Beispieltext)

Hi Jason, I am at a flea market right now. It is such fun because there is so much to look at here. There are different types of people here, like children with their parents, tourists and police officers. There are even some dogs! Right now I am walking to the food area to buy something sweet. I can see a stall selling waffles, and another is selling crepes. Getting to the food area is a challenge, people are always stopping. Whether they are talking to a seller, or looking at an item on a stall, no one here is walking fast. After I buy something to eat, I am meeting my friend Benjamin. He is buying a book right now. What are you doing right now? Bye, Markus

Language Detective

1. It was the Vikings who arrived in America hundreds of years earlier.
2. They had weapons which were very strong.
3. Their customers were people who lived all over the world.

1 Who or which?

1. who 2. which 3. who 4. which 5. who 6. who 7. which 8. who 9. which

2 At the Viking festival

1. who 2. which 3. which 4. who 5. which 6. who 7. which 8. which

3 Who or what is it?

1. The Vikings were people who sailed the seas.
2. A warrior is someone who fights in battles.
3. A beard is hair which grows on your face.
4. A mother is a woman who has got a child.
5. Costumes are clothes which you can wear.

4 This is an exercise which I like

1. A sword is a weapon which is very sharp.
2. Festival staff are people who tell you about Vikings/who work at a festival/… .
3. Food stalls are the stalls which sell burgers, fries and more/which sell food/… .
4. A selfie is a photo of you which you take of yourself.
5. A helmet is something which protects your head/which you wear on your head/… .
6. Sunday is a day which ends the week/which I like very much/… .
7. Hammers are tools which can fix things/which are very heavy/… .

Over to you (Beispieltext)

Hi Amelia!

How are you? I want to tell you about the Viking festival which I went to. I went with my dad and my brothers who didn't want to go, but when we got there they loved it! There were loads of stalls which sold Viking products. They even sold swords, which dad wouldn't let us buy, he thought they were too dangerous. There were also lots of people who were wearing Viking costumes. A man told us that the people wearing the costumes are the ones who know the most Viking facts. So, my brothers walked over to a big man who was wearing a costume and holding a sword and asked him a question. For lunch there were stalls which sold burgers, pizza and chips. There was even one stall which sold traditional Viking food, which I tried and it was horrible. Nevertheless definitely go to the Viking festival which is in your town!

Bye,

Lucy

Language Detective

Beispiele: 1. It was great.   2. They weren't really fighting.   3. Were you watching the finale too?

1   Was or were?

1. was   2. was   3. was   4. were   5. were   6. were   7. was   8. were

2   What were they doing?

1. Emma <u>was baking</u> Viking bread. She <u>was mixing</u> flour and water with her hands. People <u>were watching</u> her.
2. Justin <u>was making</u> firewood . He <u>was using</u> a hammer as a tool. He <u>was explaining</u> to the visitors what he <u>was doing</u>.
3. Sam <u>was building</u> a boat. His sister <u>was helping</u> him. She <u>was standing</u> in the background when I took the picture. Sam <u>was working</u> the wood with his tools.
4. The actor <u>was posing</u> for Talisha's picture. He <u>was wearing</u> an expensive warrior costume and he <u>was carrying</u> a sword.
5. The warriors <u>were training</u> for the battle scene at the finale. They <u>were holding</u> swords and axes. Their coach <u>was telling</u> them what to do.

3   She wasn't …

1. Talisha wasn't wearing a costume.
2. Talisha wasn't lighting fireworks.
3. Talisha wasn't filming a video.
4. Talisha wasn't eating waffles.
5. Talisha wasn't shopping at the stalls.
6. Talisha wasn't putting away her mobile phone.

4   What were you doing?

a)
1. What were you doing when your mobile phone rang?
2. Was it raining?
3. Why was your mum wearing a beard?
4. Which weapons were the Vikings using during the battle scenes?
5. Were you taking lots of pictures?

b) Beispiele:
1. What were you eating at the festival?
2. What were the Vikings fighting with?
3. Who was fighting who during the battle?
4. Which music was playing during the battle?

5   How do you say it in English?

2. The Vikings in the show were all wearing long beards.
3. She was paying for the chips when her phone rang.
4. I was looking for a bin when I saw John.
5. John was calling, but then he saw me.

Over to you (Beispieltext)

Hello, today I am going to tell you about the great day I had at the street festival parade. I went with my parents and some of their friends too. When we arrived, the atmosphere was so good! A singer was singing on the stage, there were dancers dancing too. So first we watched the concert for a while, then we saw some people that were eating, which made us hungry, so we bought burgers and chips. After that we had ice cream! My dad was taking pictures all day and he was even filming a video of all the amazing things you could watch. The parade was loud and tiring but really fun.

Language Detective

1. found 2. saw 3. did 4. fired 5. spoke 6. became 7. was 8. was able to

1 do – did

do	did		put	put		think	thought		be	was /		cross	crossed
go	went		leave	left		tell	told			were		hit	hit
get	got		make	made		sell	sold		know	knew		buy	bought
have	had		find	found		take	took		eat	ate			
stay	stayed		swim	swam		stand	stood		listen	listened			
open	opened		hear	heard		see	saw		lose	lost			

2 How a dolphin saved me

Fifty years ago my friends and I <u>were</u> on a boat trip in the Caribbean, when in the middle of the night a storm <u>hit</u>. I <u>fell</u> overboard and nobody <u>saw</u> me. But I <u>was</u> lucky because I <u>had</u> my life jacket on and I am a good swimmer, too. So I <u>swam</u> to the beach as quickly as I <u>could</u>. Then something <u>touched</u> my leg. What a scary situation. First I <u>thought</u> it was a shark, but then I <u>saw</u> that two dolphins were swimming next to me . One of them <u>helped</u> me to get to the beach. I <u>said</u>: "Thank you so much for rescuing me."

3 My friend Friday and I

1. Friday did not/didn't speak English.
2. At first, I did not/didn't understand him.
3. He was not/wasn't able to write.
4. I did not/didn't know how to fish.
5. We did not/didn't have any problems.
6. The cannibals did not/didn't find us again.
7. I was not/wasn't afraid.

4 What was the question?

2. What was his name?
3. Why did you call him Friday?
4. What did he teach you to do?
5. Where did the ship bring you?
6. Did Friday come with you?
7. Did you miss anything about the island?

5 How do you say it in English?

1. We were on a lonely island.
2. We had a problem, because we didn't have toothbrushes with us.
3. We used leaves to collect water.
4. Everyone thought we needed a knife.
5. We missed our friends so much, but it was also a great adventure.

Over to you (Beispieltext)

Hi guys! I was stranded on a desert island for 6 months last year. I will share my experiences with you, so you know what it was like. I arrived on the island because of a plane crash. I was on my way to have a holiday in Mexico, when the plane had some problems and crashed into the sea. I used a broken door to sail to an island. One day I made a fire, and started collecting fruits from a tree. I looked around and suddenly everything was on fire! At the same time, a helicopter flew over me. I shouted at it and ran around, hoping they would see me. They saw my fire! The fire was the worst and best thing that ever happened to me! They took me home and I was able to see my family again.

Language Detective

1. First you need to find some water.
2. You need something to cut plants.
3. If you don't have any matches …
4. Is there anything else you need?
5. You need to find something to build your home with.

1 What do you need on a desert island?

1. First, you need <u>something</u> to drink. This can be water or fruit juice.
2. If you don't have <u>anything</u> to eat, you have to find fruit or hunt animals on the island.
3. If you have fire, you can cook animals and heat up water to clean it. Don't eat or drink <u>anything</u> that is dirty!
4. You also need <u>something</u> to clean your teeth with so that they don't go bad.
5. On an island, you will find <u>something</u> to build a small house with. You need a shelter.
6. You can use wood, for example, and <u>something</u> soft and long to put it together so that it becomes a small house.

2 Alone on the island

Let me tell you <u>something</u> about my biggest adventure ever. There I was, alone on an island. The good thing was that I had a knife and <u>some</u> matches, but I didn't have <u>anything</u> to drink. So I looked around to see if I could find <u>any</u> water. First, I couldn't find <u>any</u> water. Then I saw <u>some</u> coconuts. I opened them with my knife and drank the coconut water. On the second day I was lucky. I found a little river. I took <u>some</u> of the water with me. I could also see <u>some</u> fish. I had not eaten <u>anything</u> that day yet. I tried to catch one of them. It was very difficult, and I didn't catch <u>any</u> at all. I had to practise. I looked for <u>some</u> sticks and I sharpened them with my knife. After two days eating only coconuts I actually caught a fish. I had to eat it without <u>any</u> salt, but it was better than nothing! Later I also learnt how to collect <u>some</u> water with leaves.

3 How do you say it in English?

1. Tia, do we have anything else to drink?
2. Wir haben kein Kokoswasser mehr, aber Tia hat vorhin etwas Wasser in den Blättern gefunden. Also ja.
3. Tia, do you want anything to eat? We have fish and red fruits.
4. Marcel, Tia möchte etwas zu essen, sie ist sehr hungrig. Kannst du ihr auch etwas über diese Insel erzählen?
5. Tia, unfortunately he doesn't know anything about the island, but he has never seen anything more beautiful.

Over to you (Beispieltext)

Dear diary,

There is something I need to tell you. I have now been stuck on this island for a whole week. Today I went to look for some water, because it didn't rain last night so there wasn't any water on the leaves, but I could hear something far away, which sounded like water. I walked towards it for a really long time, and I couldn't see anything. Then suddenly I saw a huge river. Then I realised I did not have anything to hold the water in. I made a cup from a leaf and drank it. Now I need something to eat. There were some plants that you can eat next to the river. "I need something to cut them with" I thought. Then I remembered the knife I keep in my pocket. The leaves tasted bad, but they were better than being hungry.

Language Detective

1. If they stop arguing 2. if they buy a dog. 3. If you play with a little dog 4. If they go out with the dog

1 If it rains …

1. If it **rains** / ~~will rain~~ on Sunday, we **will stay** / ~~stay~~ at home.
2. If the weather **is** / ~~will be~~ good, I **will go** / ~~go~~ skateboarding.
3. My dad ~~makes~~ / **will make** breakfast tomorrow if he **gets up** / ~~will get up~~ early.
4. I **will do** / ~~do~~ my homework later if I ~~will go~~ / **go** skateboarding now.
5. If my grandparents **visit** / ~~will visit~~ us, it ~~is~~ / **will be** lots of fun.
6. If we **play** / ~~will play~~ board games together, my grandma ~~wins~~ / **will win**.
7. If my bike **is** / ~~will be~~ broken, I ~~take~~ / **will take** the bus to school.

2 Solving problems

1. If my dad needs help making pancakes, I will show him how to do it.
2. If the weather is bad, Peter will stay inside and play games.
3. If I come home very late, I will get in trouble with my parents.
4. If our dog Bello wants to go outside, we will take him for a walk.
5. If my sister can't do her homework, my mum will help her.
6. If my mum tells me to tidy up, I will tell her I have to do my homework.

3 More problems

2. I will be able to do the school project if you help me.
3. You will get a bad cold if you don't wear a warm jacket.
4. Your teammates will understand if you don't come to the match.
5. Everybody will be happy if you bring cake to school.
6. You will be in trouble with Mr Jenkins if you do not do your English homework.

4 Sentence chain

a)
2. If you are hungry at school, you will not be able to concentrate on your schoolwork.
3. If you are not able to concentrate on your schoolwork, your schoolwork will not be so good.
4. If your schoolwork isn't so good, you will feel stressed out.
5. If you feel stressed out, you will be unhappy.
b) Beispiel: If you are unhappy, you won't enjoy your free time.

5 How do you say it in English?

1. If he doesn't do his homework, he will get in trouble.
2. If you do not stop arguing, I will go home.
3. Will I get some pocket money if I clean the car?
4. If I am not allowed to watch the film, I will listen to music.
5. If we go to the cinema today, we will see James Bond.

Over to you (Beispieltext)

Hi Claudia! How are you? I want to tell you today about a problem I have. I keep getting bad marks at school. Every time I take a test, I get a bad mark, even when I try really hard. So here is my plan. I hope if I play less video games, I will go to bed earlier. Then, if I go to bed earlier, I will wake up more easily and I will be less tired. If I am less tired at school, I will concentrate better, and if I concentrate better, I will understand the work more. So, I will play less video games to concentrate more at school. Bye, Elton

Language Detective

I	myself		he	himself		it	itself		you	yourselves
you	yourself		she	herself		we	ourselves		they	themselves

1 I like myself.

1. I like myself.
2. Justin, you like yourself.
3. My sister likes herself.
4. My sister and I like ourselves.
5. My dad likes himself.
6. You two like yourselves.
7. Bill and Bob like themselves.
8. Jenny and Mia like themselves.
9. We like ourselves.
10. The robot likes itself.

2 Be careful about what you post!

Hi everyone! I am Brenda. I would like to give you some tips about how to stay safe online and also tell you something about how I made a big mistake myself. Here is the thing: Don't post any embarrassing photos of yourself online. Never! Lisa, one of my friends, recently posted a picture of herself in funny clothes and she was very sad about all the bad comments she got. When Peter repaired his bike himself, he posted a short video about how he did it. It was just a normal vlog, but he still got weird comments. We all post things on social media and some time later we are very unhappy that there are photos of ourselves online. I mean, the internet doesn't forget! Actually, I put a really stupid photo of myself online once. My mum saw it and was very angry at herself because she was the one who allowed me to use social media. People can enjoy themselves on social media. We all just have to be careful about what we want to share with the world. One last thing: Don't ever feel bad about yourself because of pictures you saw online. Mostly, people use filters and are not just themselves.

3 How do you say it in German?

1. Oje! Ich habe mich geschnitten.
2. Die Katze wäscht sich oft.
3. Wir gehen auf die Party und amüsieren uns.
4. Jane betrachtet sich im Spiegel.
5. Fühle dich nicht schlecht wegen der Bilder, die du online siehst.

Over to you (Beispieltext)

Hi Leo! Guess what: my parents are away for the weekend. That means we are all by ourselves, except when my grandma comes to our house to check we are OK. Yesterday was the first morning we were alone. Usually, we like to wake up late, but instead we forced ourselves to get up so we could have as much time alone as possible. Me and my sister made ourselves waffles which were delicious. Mum doesn't let us have them, she says "you will eat too many and make yourselves sick." But I was fine, and I enjoyed myself. Then we had an idea! Mum and dad have gone away because it is mum's birthday, we should make her a cake, she can eat it all by herself! I am bad at making cakes so I let my siblings do it themselves, meanwhile I watched the cat clean itself. Then grandma came to the house and we watched a film, I liked being by myself but I am happy that mum and dad are coming back tonight, I hope they enjoyed themselves.

Language Detective

1. He was bought in the 1920's.
2. His eyes were taken out.
3. Charles was taken good care of.
4. He was found again.
5. Lots of great things are invented.

1 Past participle

break	broken	forget	forgot/forgotten	show	shown
catch	caught	keep	kept	take	taken
cut	cut	know	known		
find	found	pay	paid		

2 Facts about inventions

1. made 2. sold 3. put 4. used 5. found 6. eaten

3 Inventions at home

1. was bought 2. was stolen 3. was put 4. were uploaded 5. was invented 6. was made 7. were built

4 Getting the facts right

1. It was invented by Thomas Edison.
2. They are used to heat up food.
3. They are brought to school by car.
4. They are put on letters.

5 It was written by ...

2. One of the first computers was called "Baby".
3. More than 120 million smartphones were bought in 2007.
4. The guitar is played all over the world.
5. Sushi is not only eaten in Japan.

6 From active to passive

2. The first text message was sent in 1992.
3. Video games are played all over the world.
4. Muesli is usually eaten with milk.
5. The Sherlock Holmes stories were written more than a hundred years ago by Sir Arthur Conan Doyle.

Over to you (Beispieltext)

Hi everyone,

Today I am going to tell you all about my favourite invention ever! It is the video game console! The first console was invented in the early 1970's. It was called the Magnavox Odyssey. A table tennis game could be played on it, which would not seem very fun to us today! But back then it was amazing. Other games included Ski, Tennis, Cat and mouse and Haunted house. It cost around $99 in 1972, which would be equal to about $550 in today's money. I am so happy that my console cost so much less than that. The design of the console was developed and perfected over the years. I love my games console because I can play on it instead of doing my homework!

Jack

Language Detective

simple past: **Verb** + - **ed** oder irreguläres **Verb**   present perfect: have / has + **Verb** + - **ed** oder irreguläres **Verb**

1   Signal words

simple past	present perfect
yesterday, last week, two years ago, last winter, in 1995	already, not…yet, never

2   At the station

2. The train ~~did already leave~~. We will have to wait for the next one.   has already left
3. I ~~did never hear~~ this song before. It's great!   have never heard
4. Why ~~haven't you been~~ on the train ten minutes ago?   weren't you
5. I ~~have gone~~ to Wales last year.   went
6. I am so bored. The train ~~didn't arrive~~ yet.   hasn't arrived

3   Holidays

Oliver: Hi Brendon! My name is Oliver. Nice to meet you. That is a picture of Edinburgh, isn't it? <u>Have you ever been</u> to Scotland?

Brendon: Yes, I <u>have</u>. I <u>went</u> there last year with my family. We <u>visited</u> Edinburgh and <u>had</u> lots of fun.

Oliver: <u>Did you see</u> Edinburgh Castle, too?

Brendon: Yes, we <u>did</u>. We <u>found</u> it really interesting. Last year we only <u>stayed</u> in Edinburgh. I <u>have never been</u> to the Highlands. That's still on my list. I <u>have never seen</u> any of the Lochs.

Oliver: Well, will you go back to Scotland soon?

Brendon: I don't know. My parents said because we <u>have already been</u> to Scotland, we should go somewhere else this year like Italy or Germany. We <u>haven't decided</u> yet

Oliver: Germany sounds nice. I <u>have never been</u> there.

4   Which one is it?

1. I have already bought the tickets.
2. I went to Wales last year.
3. The train arrived an hour ago.
4. Yesterday I lost my phone.
5. Have you ever milked a highland cow?
6. Did you go to the cinema last week?
7. When did you go to Spain?

5   How do you say it in English?

1. Have you ever been to Brighton?
2. Where did you go last year?
3. Has the train already left?
4. I haven't bought a bottle of water yet.
5. Did he miss the train yesterday?

Over to you (Beispieltext)

Hi everyone! Today I am going to talk to you about the holiday I went on. My parents come from Greece, so I went to visit my grandparents there. We go there every two years, and in between they come to London to see us! This year the week we went was the same week as the village festival. It was amazing. There were so many things to do. We usually eat the food my grandma makes when we are in Greece, so I have never actually been to a Greek restaurant. So when mum said we could get food from the festival I was so excited. We ate probably the most famous Greek food there is – Gyros. Have you ever tried it? It is delicious. It is meat, chips, salad and a garlic sauce inside of a pita bread! Later that week we did a road trip to the coast of Greece to go to the beach, I have never seen a beach so beautiful! The sand was white and the water was clear. Have you ever been to Greece? Bye, Andreas.

Language Detective

1. I secretly hoped that we would see the famous monster.
2. Everything happened so quickly.

3. We drove off as quickly as we could.

1 Holidays in Scotland

1. fast 2. angrily 3. cutely 4. hard 5. hungrily 6. beautifully

2 Adverbs

beautiful	beautifully
terrible	terribly
bad	badly
loud	loudly

slow	slowly
good	well
short	shortly
happy	happily

easy	easily
hard	hard

3 Adjective or adverb?

When we arrived in Scotland, it was raining ~~heavy~~ / **heavily**. Our hotel is very **nice** / ~~nicely~~. On our first day here we slept very ~~good~~ / **well**. My parents wanted to visit Urquart Castle. They were talking about it ~~excited~~ / **excitedly**. I wasn't very **excited** / ~~excitedly~~, because I don't really like old castles. I think they are **boring** / ~~boringly~~. On our trip there the sun was shining ~~bright~~ / **brightly**. Then we drove past a **beautiful** / ~~beautifully~~ lake. It was the **famous** / ~~famously~~ Loch Ness. The water sparkled ~~beautiful~~ / **beautifully** in the sun. My brother Josh and I ~~secret~~ / **secretly** hoped to see the monster. "There it is!" Josh said ~~loud~~ / **loudly**. There was no monster, of course. My brother just thought it was **funny** / ~~funnily~~.

4 How do you say it in English?

1. He quickly went back to the hotel.
2. She spoke slowly and very quietly.
3. The three dogs barked quite loudly.

4. It rained heavily.
5. The fish quickly disappeared.

Over to you (Beispieltext)

My family went to Scotland last year for our summer holiday. The weather was dark, and the rain fell heavily over us as we walked around the Loch. Despite the weather, it was breathtaking. My brother sighed tiredly as we stopped to look at the view. Suddenly a bolt of lightning struck and the whole lake and sky looked black. We all saw the head of Nessie coming out of the water. My brother shouted "It's Nessie, run!" We all hurried frantically to the car. Mum drove the car wildly away from the Loch. When we got back to the hotel, we were exhausted. A lady asked us curiously what we had done that day. We all talked at once, answering her question enthusiastically.

"You saw the Loch Ness Monster?" She said in disbelieve. "Don't be silly, she doesn't exist."

BILDQUELLEN

infinitive	simple past	past participle	Deutsch
be	was/were	been	sein
beat	beat	beaten	schlagen; besiegen
become	became	become	werden
begin	began	begun	anfangen; beginnen
bite	bit	bitten	beißen
break	broke	broken	(zer)brechen; kaputtgehen
bring	brought	brought	(mit)bringen
build	built	built	bauen
buy	bought	bought	kaufen
catch	caught	caught	fangen
choose	chose	chosen	auswählen
come	came	come	kommen
cost	cost	cost	kosten
cry	cried	cried	schreien; weinen
cut	cut	cut	schneiden
dig	dug	dug	graben
do	did	done	machen, tun
draw	drew	drawn	zeichnen
drink	drank	drunk	trinken
drive	drove	driven	fahren
eat	ate	eaten	essen
fall	fell	fallen	fallen
feed	fed	fed	füttern, zu Essen geben
feel	felt	felt	(sich) fühlen
fight	fought	fought	(be)kämpfen; streiten
find	found	found	finden
fit	fit/fitted	fit/fitted	passen (zu)
fly	flew	flown	fliegen
forget	forgot	forgotten	vergessen
forgive	forgave	forgiven	vergeben, verzeihen
get	got	got/gotten	erhalten, bekommen; werden

IRREGULAR VERBS

infinitive	simple past	past participle	Deutsch
give	gave	given	geben
go	went	gone	gehen; fahren
grow	grew	grown	wachsen; anbauen
hang	hung	hung	(auf)hängen
have	had	had	haben; essen
hear	heard	heard	hören
hide	hid	hidden	(sich) verstecken
hit	hit	hit	schlagen; treffen
hold	held	held	(fest)halten
keep	kept	kept	(be)halten; aufbewahren
know	knew	known	wissen; kennen
lay	laid	laid	legen; hinlegen
lead	led	led	(an)führen, leiten
learn	learnt/learned	learnt/learned	lernen
leave	left	left	verlassen; hinterlassen;
let	let	let	lassen
light	lit	lit	erhellen; anzünden
lose	lost	lost	verlieren
make	made	made	machen; ergeben
mean	meant	meant	bedeuten; meinen
meet	met	met	(sich) treffen; kennenlernen
pay	paid	paid	(be)zahlen
put	put	put	setzen, legen, stellen
read	read	read	lesen
rebuild	rebuilt	rebuilt	wieder aufbauen
ride	rode	ridden	fahren; reiten
ring	rang	rung	klingeln; läuten
rise	rose	risen	(auf)steigen; sich erheben
run	ran	run	laufen, rennen; funktionieren
say	said	said	sagen
see	saw	seen	sehen

infinitive	simple past	past participle	Deutsch
sell	sold	sold	verkaufen
send	sent	sent	(zu)schicken; ver-/absenden
shine	shone	shone	scheinen, leuchten
shoot	shot	shot	(er)schießen
show	showed	shown	zeigen
sing	sang	sung	singen
sit	sat	sat	sitzen
sleep	slept	slept	schlafen
speak	spoke	spoken	sprechen, reden
spell	spelt/spelled	spelt/spelled	buchstabieren
spend	spent	spent	ausgeben (Geld); verbringen (Zeit)
split	split	split	spalten; teilen
stand	stood	stood	stehen; ertragen, aushalten
steal	stole	stolen	stehlen, klauen
stick	stuck	stuck	kleben
stink	stank/stunk	stunk	stinken
swim	swam	swum	schwimmen
take	took	taken	(mit)nehmen; bringen; brauchen, dauern
teach	taught	taught	unterrichten; beibringen
tell	told	told	erzählen; sagen
think	thought	thought	denken, glauben, meinen
throw	threw	thrown	werfen
try	tried	tried	(aus)probieren; versuchen
understand	understood	understood	verstehen
wear	wore	worn	tragen (Kleidung)
win	won	won	gewinnen
write	wrote	written	schreiben